Praise for *Truffles, Candies & Confections*

"Chocoholics, rejoice! Ms. Bloom is an excellent instructor, so virtually all of her recipes can be duplicated with relative ease."

—*The Atlanta Journal-Constitution*

"This will remain the standard for years to come."

—*World of Cookbooks*

"A great find for cooks wanting to give a really grand treat as a holiday gift."

—*The Columbus Dispatch*

"Carole Bloom has created the most mouth-watering, "user-friendly" recipes I've seen in a long time! The crystal-clear instructions will instill confidence in novice candymakers, and inspire experienced chocolatiers."

—Rick Rodgers, author of *Best-Ever Chocolate Desserts* and *Best-Ever Brownies*

"At last there is a step-by-step guide to creating elegant candies at home. Carol includes an equipment list, instruction on techniques and a delightful collection of her favorite candy recipes. From Cappucino Truffles to Marzipan Chocolate Squares, *Truffles, Candies, & Confections* is a must for all home candymakers."

—Janie Hibler, author of *Dungeness Crabs & Blackberry Cobblers* and *Game Cookery*

"I thought no chocolate truffles could compare with my French grandmother's. None that is, until I sampled a few of Carole Bloom's meltingly-smooth concoctions: And there they were, real 'truffles au chocolat' just like my grandmother used to make!"

—Kitty Morse, author of *Come with me to the Kasbah: A Cook's Tour of Morocco* and a columnist with the *Los Angeles Times* North County Focus

"Carole Bloom's clear instructions and tempting recipes will turn ordinary cooks into accomplished confectioners."

—Nick Malgieri, author of *Perfect Pastry* and *Great Italian Desserts*

Truffles, Candies, & Confections

Elegant Candymaking in the Home

by

Carole Bloom

Photography by Glenn Cormier

THE CROSSING PRESS, FREEDOM, CA 95019

Photo Credits

Chocolate Hearts: Nancy Calhoun Designs Lacquer Ware Charger, The Dining Room Shop, La Jolla, CA.

Hazelnut Chocolate Tuiles: Marble rolling pin, The Kitchen Witch Gourmet Shop, Encinitas, CA. Enamel on copper Bowl by Barbara Culp, Bo Danica, La Jolla, CA.

Chocolate Nut Bark: Handmade green plate by Barbara Eigen, Bo Danica, La Jolla, CA.

White Chocolate Apricot Truffles: Villeroy & Bach Marbled Charger and Marguerite Box, Jan Bos Meyers.

English Toffee: Nancy Calhoun Designs Lacquer Ware Charger and handmade Gold Rimmed Glass Plate by Annie Glass, The Dining Room Shop, La Jolla, CA.

Turtles: Sumi gold rimmed plates designed & hand painted by A. Mallory, Bo Danica, La Jolla, CA.

Hazelnut Chocolate Truffles: Enamel on Copper Platter by Barbara Culp and hand painted paper box by Wood Expressions, Bo Danica, La Jolla, CA.

Gold Disks: Taitù Italian Plate, The Dining Room Shop, La Jolla, CA.

Classic Chocolate Truffles: Gold Ribbon, Jan Bos Meyers.

Horizontal Group: Solstice Gold Leaf Trivet, Bo Danica, La Jolla, CA.

All other props are privately owned.

Copyright © 1992 by Carole Bloom
Cover Design by AnneMarie Arnold
Photographs Copyright © 1992 by Glenn Cormier
Photographic Styling by Margaret Daley
Food Styling by Carole Bloom
Book Design by Amy Sibiga, AnneMarie Arnold and Sheryl Karas
Illustrations Copyright © 1992 by Amy Sibiga
Printed in Singapore
First Edition

Second Edition, paperback.1996
Bloom, Carole.
Truffles, candies & confections: elegant candymaking in the home/
by Carole Bloom.
      p.   cm.
Includes index
ISBN 0-89594-559-2
1. Candy. I. Title. II. Title: Truffles, candies, and confections.
TX791.B56 1992
641.8'53--dc20   92-2256
                                                CIP

*This book is dedicated with love to my
husband, Jerry, and to my mother and
the memory of my father.*

My biggest thanks go to my husband, Jerry Olivas, who is a constant source of support, help, and encouragement. He is always there for me no matter where I am. During the writing of this book he ran to the store for a needed ingredient, washed dishes and cleaned up the kitchen after a busy day of recipe testing, and, certainly, tasted the day's work. His creativity is an inspiration and he has a great flair for finding just the right word when needed. Also, his computer knowledge is invaluable. Without his help and support throughout the process, this book would not exist.

A big thank-you goes to my good friend and colleague Pam Wischkaemper, who helped me to be in the right place at the right time. A simple invitation to attend a luncheon led me to find the publisher for this book. Thanks, also, to Michael Wischkaemper for his legal savvy.

Thanks to my dear friends and colleagues Lily Loh and Kitty Morse for their constant encouragement, and for letting me bend their ears and use their shoulders to lean on when needed. Thanks, also, to Betz Collins for her valuable suggestions and to Steve de Leau for supplying me with superb chocolate.

Many thanks to my good friend Jan Bos Meyers for letting me use many beautiful items from her tabletop collections for the photographs. Also, my sincere appreciation and admiration goes to Glenn Cormier and Margaret Daley for producing the beautiful photographs for this book.

My mother, Florence Bloom, is excited about my work and brags about me to all her friends. Thanks, Mom! My father, Milton Bloom, always believed that I could do anything I wanted to do. He was a great candy lover. If he were here, he would be very pleased to see this book.

Special thanks to Barbara Feller-Roth, my editor, for her enthusiastic support and constant attention to detail. She was a pleasure to work with and did a superb job.

Contents

Working with Chocolate... Kneading Marzipan... Working with Nuts... Measuring Dry Ingredients... Packing Candies and Confections for Gifts and to Mail... Pastry Bag Techniques... Paper Pastry Cones... Using a Zester... Do-Ahead Tips

Classic Chocolate... Swiss Chocolate... Raspberry... Hazelnut Chocolate... Orange Chocolate... Tea... Mocha... Cappucino... Gianduja... Italian Gianduja... California... Gold Disks... White Chocolate Apricot... Tropical... Macadamia Nut... White Chocolate Ginger... Gianduja Cups... Mocha Ganache Cups... Hazelnut Ganache Cups

Orange Hazelnut Chocolate Clusters... Chocolate Peanut Clusters... Rochers... Tropical Clusters... Hazelnut Chocolate Tuiles... Chocolate Nut Bark... Gianduja Diamonds... Gianduja Bars... California Fruit & Nut Chocolate Bars... Nougatine Triangles... Nutella Surprises... Hazelnut Chocolate Kisses... Chocolate Almond Cups... Extraordinary Candy Bars... Chocolate Hearts

Introduction

This book is about pleasure. The pleasure of making and eating truffles, candies, and confections. Anyone can go to the store and buy something to satisfy their craving for candy. But what is bought most likely has been mass produced—it won't be fresh, it will have been made with artificial additives, and it won't taste anywhere as good as if it were homemade. The recipes in this book make it easy and fun to make what may well be the most delicious homemade truffles, candies, and confections you have ever eaten.

When it comes to eating something sweet, candy tops the list for most people, myself included. I have fond childhood memories of buying and eating candy from the neighborhood candy store. Standing in front of the counter and trying to make a choice was difficult, but fun. The clear glass shelves were stocked with all manner of candies—some wrapped in colorful foil, some stacked high on trays, some glistening in jars. My favorite candies were round red licorice coins. They were chewy and lasted a long time. As I got older my tastes changed, and chocolate became my great love, the darker the better.

My professional experience in the culinary field began in the early 1970s as I was completing my bachelor of arts degree in fine arts from the University of California, Berkeley. I worked as a cook in several small gourmet restaurants in Berkeley. Although I enjoyed all types of cooking, I especially liked making desserts. I decided that I would specialize in desserts and traveled to Europe to study and work.

In Switzerland I saw and ate some of the world's finest truffles, candies, and confections, and I was determined to create them myself. One confectionery shop that really excited me was Sprüngli in Zurich. Everything in their display windows is picture perfect and everything tastes as good as it looks.

As a pastry chef, I perfected the art of making these delights. I have been able to share these skills during the last twelve years of teaching classes on truffles, candies, and confections. I have taught my students how to easily and quickly make wonderful sweets. I stress the need to use the best ingredients and equipment, and the correct techniques. My students have praised me for the clarity of my recipes and for teaching them the simplest way to create the best.

The difference between truffles, candies, and confections can be confusing. These terms are related and often used interchangeably. A truffle is a type of candy or confection, with a soft chocolate center surrounded by an outer coating of either chocolate, cocoa powder, or chopped nuts. Candy usually refers to brittles, toffees, and other hard sweets, whereas confections can be thought of as a general category of sweets, other than truffles and hard candies. However, the word *confection* is commonly used in reference to truffles, candies, and a host of other sweet treats. This includes molded candies, caramels, marzipan, fudges, nougats, divinity, candied fruits, and other fruit candies. One similarity that truffles, candies, and confections have in common, is that all except for candy bars are small enough to be consumed in one or two bites. Also, all are sweetened in some way, usually with sugar.

The art of making candies and confections is an ancient one. Honey was the first sweetener, used long before sugar. The Crusaders brought sugar back with them from their journeys to the Holy Land in the early Middle Ages. It was a highly prized substance, which did not come into widespread use until the early seventeenth century. It's interesting to note that the word *candy* comes from the Arabic word for sugar, *qand*.

When making candies and confections, always be sure to read the entire recipe first so that you will know what ingredients and equipment are necessary, and what techniques are to be used. It is a good idea to measure out all the ingredients, and set out all the equipment, before beginning to prepare the recipe. Proportions are very important, so be sure to measure ingredients accurately.

Chapter 1 discusses several major ingredients that are used throughout the book. Chapter 2 provides information on equipment and tools. Some of these may be new to you, although you probably already have most of what you need in your kitchen. Chapter 3 discusses various techniques used in many recipes throughout the book. Recipes calling for a particular technique refer you to the page in Chapter 3 where the technique is described. There are six recipe chapters beginning with Chapter 4, Truffles. The procedures for making all truffles are similar, so once you have made one recipe, it will be easy to make the others. Chapter 5, More Chocolate Candies, covers chocolate candies other than truffles. Many variations are offered with these recipes, so there is something for everyone. Several different recipes for caramels, including the all-time favorite, Turtles, are in Chapter 6, Caramel Candies. For nut lovers, Chapter 7, Nut Brittles and Marzipan, offers a variety of crunchy choices. Several recipes and variations for Fudge, Nougat, and Divinity are in Chapter 8. These recipes are classic favorites. The recipe chapters conclude with Chapter 9, Fruit Candies. These candies offer the zesty flavor of both fresh and dried fruit.

Two Appendices are at the end of the book. The Table of Sugar Stages and Temperatures and the Table of Weight and Measurement Equivalents are for reference, as needed.

It is fun and creative to make truffles, candies, and confections on your own, but group candymaking can be even more fun. This is a great way for family and friends to get together for a good time and to enjoy some delicious goodies. It is an ideal way to introduce children to the tradition of family candymaking.

Candies, especially homemade candies, are the ultimate gift. Receiving a choice selection of handmade candies in an attractive box or tin is a delight of the holiday season and Valentine's Day as well. What better way to say "I love you" than with a gift from your kitchen, made with love and care.

Little kids, big kids, and adults of all ages love truffles, candies, and confections. Most people have to settle for store-bought, a pale imitation. Why not have the real thing? I invite you to experience the enjoyment of making your own truffles, candies, and confections. They will probably be the best you have ever eaten!

Ingredients

*T*o create the best-tasting truffles, candies, and confections always use the best-quality ingredients. They are easy to find and not much more expensive than average-quality ingredients. If a poor-quality ingredient is used, such as imitation chocolate, its flavor cannot be disguised.

All of the ingredients used in this book are readily available in supermarkets, specialty food shops, cookware stores, and from mail order sources.

Butter

Unsalted butter is used in all the recipes in this book that require butter. Salt was originally added to butter as a preservative. When using salted butter, it is difficult to tell how much salt is in the butter, since different brands use different amounts of salt, so it is hard to judge how much salt should be added to each recipe. Unsalted butter has a fresher flavor and less water than regular butter. It tends to spoil more easily, so it should be kept in the freezer if it needs to be stored longer than a week. Be sure to wrap it well so it does not pick up other flavors. Using margarine in place of butter will noticeably effect the flavor of the finished confections.

Candy Coffee Beans

Used for decoration, these commercially produced candies are shaped like coffee beans and taste like coffee. There are also candy mocha beans that look like candy coffee beans but have a mocha flavor.

Chocolate

Chocolate is derived from cocoa beans that grow in large pods on trees. The scientific name for the cocoa tree is *Theobroma*, which comes from Greek and means "food of the gods." Cocoa trees grow in countries that are close to the equator. The pods are cut from the trees and split open, then the beans are removed and left to dry and ferment in the sun for a few days before being packed for shipping.

Upon arrival at the chocolate factory, the cocoa beans are roasted at a temperature between 250°F and 350°F for approximately 1 hour. During this process the outer hulls of the cocoa beans split open. These hulls are discarded, leaving the inner nib, the kernel, which contains the essence of chocolate. These nibs are ground, producing a liquid called chocolate liquor, which is the basis of all chocolates. When the liquid, called cocoa butter, is extracted from chocolate liquor, the powder that remains is cocoa powder. Cocoa powder tends to be acid. Adding alkali to it produces a mellow flavor. This process was discovered by a Dutchman and is known as Dutch-processed cocoa. It produces the richest and most flavorful cocoa.

Types of Chocolate. Bitter chocolate or unsweetened chocolate is pure chocolate liquor with the addition of vanilla. To make semisweet and bittersweet chocolate, cocoa butter is added back to the chocolate liquor, with sugar, vanilla, and lecithin. The difference between semisweet and bittersweet chocolate is the amount of added sugar. For milk chocolate, milk solids are also added. White chocolate is composed of cocoa butter, milk solids, sugar, vanilla, and lecithin. After blending these ingredients, the mixture is "conched," or stirred, for several hours. How long chocolate is conched depends on the brand. High-quality chocolates are conched for as long as 72 hours; some lesser-quality chocolates are conched for as little as 4 hours. This conching process is what makes chocolate smooth and creamy, and gives it its characteristic melt-in-the-mouth quality.

Since white chocolate contains no cocoa liquor, the FDA (United States Food and Drug Administration) has ruled that technically it cannot be called chocolate. It is usually labeled "confectioners' coating." Be aware that there is also a product available called "summer coating" or "compound coating," which has vegetable fat, not cocoa butter, as its base. Summer coating has a higher melting point than chocolate and does not need to be tempered, which makes it easy to handle in warm weather. Summer coating does not taste like real chocolate since it lacks cocoa butter.

Generally, semisweet and bittersweet chocolate are interchangeable in recipes. It is usually a matter of preference. Milk chocolate and white chocolate are not interchangeable with semisweet and bittersweet chocolate, because they contain milk solids and less cocoa liquor than the dark chocolates.

There is also a type of chocolate called "coverture." It has a higher percentage of cocoa butter than regular chocolate, which makes it ideal for the thin and smooth coatings for dipped truffles and candies. Coverture must be tempered to stabilize the cocoa butter (see pages 24, 29, 31). Coverture is what professional confectioners use. Available through cookware shops and mail-order supply sources, coverture can be used for the outer coating, and the filling, for any of the recipes for truffles, candies, and confections in this book. However, tempered regular chocolate will work well for dipping and coating.

What distinguishes different brands of chocolate is the recipe used by the various manufacturers. These recipes are very closely guarded secrets. Different cocoa beans are blended in various quantities, the amount of added cocoa butter varies, and the amount and types of flavorings vary, as do the length of time of roasting, grinding, and conching.

The Europeans, particularly the Swiss, were the early pioneers in producing chocolate; they perfected the art of making chocolate. Generally, European chocolates are the best tasting. The brand of chocolate I use most often is Callebaut (Belgian). Other brands I like and use occasionally are Lindt (Swiss), Tobler (Swiss), Cocoa Berry (French), Valrhona (French), Ghirardelli (American), and Guittard (American).

Choosing Chocolate. The best way to choose chocolate is to taste it. If you like the way it tastes "just plain," then you will like the way it tastes in your truffles, candies, and confections. The flavor of chocolate won't change in the process of candymaking.

Storing Chocolate. Do not store bulk chocolate in the refrigerator or freezer. It will pick up moisture from condensation, which will mix with the chocolate as it melts. Chocolate should be stored at room temperature, wrapped in foil or brown paper, not plastic wrap, which holds moisture. Dark chocolate has an indefinite shelf life. Milk chocolate and white chocolate, because of their milk solids content, have a short shelf life, between 10 months and 1 year. Be sure to buy these in small quantities and use them rapidly. Anything that is rancid smells unpleasant, so if you detect a bad odor from your chocolate, don't use it.

If chocolate becomes too warm during storage, you may notice a dull, gray film on the surface. This is known as chocolate "bloom." The cocoa butter in the emulsion has begun to separate and float to the surface. This does not mean that your chocolate has spoiled, it merely looks unpleasant. When the chocolate is melted, the cocoa butter will melt in.

If there is chocolate left after dipping truffles or candies, simply transfer it to a clean bowl, cover, and store it at room temperature. If no other substances have mixed with the chocolate, it is still pure and can be chopped and melted again. Even if the chocolate has been tempered, once it cools it is no longer in temper, and it must be tempered again before use.

Cream

Cream comes from the fat that rises to the top of unhomogenized milk. Whipping cream that has approximately 32 to 36 percent butterfat is used in all the recipes in this book that call for cream. Heavy whipping cream has a higher percentage of butterfat than regular whipping cream. It is not necessary to use heavy whipping cream for these recipes. It is best to use pasteurized cream rather than ultrapasteurized, which is heated to so high a temperature that the flavor is virtually destroyed. Be sure to pay attention to the date on the carton and use the cream before this date for guaranteed freshness.

Cream of Tartar

This is a by-product of the wine-making industry. Adding cream of tartar while beating egg whites creates the same chemical reaction that occurs when egg whites are beaten in an unlined copper bowl. This reaction allows the egg whites to reach maximum volume and keeps them from drying out. Adding cream of tartar to sugar as it is cooking helps to prevent crystallization.

Espresso Powder

For coffee flavor I always use instant espresso powder, which makes a very rich, full-bodied coffee. By using such a concentrated mixture, only a small amount of liquid needs to be added to a recipe. I like Medaglia D'oro.

Extracts

Be sure to use only pure extracts, not imitation. The imitation extracts taste like chemicals, from which they are made, and they will taint the flavor of your candies. Pure extracts are made from concentrated natural oils mixed with alcohol. Be sure to read the label, which should state that the extract is pure. Store extracts in a cool, dry place and make sure that they are tightly capped to prevent evaporation.

Gianduja

Pronounced john-DO-ya, this is a mixture of chocolate and hazelnuts. Generally milk chocolate is used, but semisweet chocolate is not uncommon. *Gianduja* chocolate has a unique flavor and a velvety smooth texture. It is used extensively in confections in Europe, where it is very popular, and is becoming more easily available in the United States. It has a short shelf life, between 6 and 8 months. One extra note should be made regarding gianduja. Although it is primarily thought of as a blended chocolate, the name gianduja also refers to confections that contain chocolate and hazelnuts.

Gold Leaf

Edible gold leaf is between 22 and 24 karat. Be sure to buy the real thing, so that it is not toxic. It is available at art supply stores and where sign-making supplies are sold and is generally available in packages of 25 leaves, arranged between sheets of tissue paper. There are two types of gold leaf, patent and loose. Patent is thick and must be cut with a knife or scissors. The loose variety is thin and works best for decorating and candymaking. Gold leaf will dissolve easily from the moisture in your hands. Handle it with a natural-bristle brush, such as sable. Touch the brush to the gold leaf, which acts like a magnet, then gently touch the gold leaf to the surface where you want it placed. Store gold leaf in a cool, dry place.

Liqueurs

Liqueurs are made from brandy or alcohol with added sugar and flavorings. Fruit brandies, or *eaux de vie*, are made from fermented distilled fruit. Liqueurs add flavor to and enhance the flavor of truffles, candies, and confections. Only a small amount is needed. Be sure to use the best quality, the same as you would drink. If you are unsure about the flavor of a liqueur, taste it before using to make sure that it is the flavor you want. Store liqueurs in a cool, dry place and make sure that they are tightly capped to prevent excess evaporation.

Nutella

This Italian product is made from hazelnuts, sugar, cocoa, and oil, and has a spreadable consistency. Nutella comes in jars and is available in the Italian specialty food section of markets and delicatessens, and in cookware shops. Nutella is used in making candy and pastry and is often used to create the unmistakable flavor of gianduja.

Nuts

Many different nuts are used in candymaking to provide both flavor and texture. All nuts have a high content of natural oil, which tends to go rancid easily. It is best to store nuts in the freezer whether they are raw, toasted, or ground. Put them in tightly covered containers or wrap them well in plastic bags. Stored this way, nuts can keep up to 1 year. Let them sit at room temperature briefly before using, or defrost them in a microwave oven.

Sugar and Other Sweeteners

Sugar imparts sweetness to candies and confections, it enhances other flavors, and adds color. Cane sugar is the type of sweetener most frequently used for candymaking, although a variety of other sweeteners are also used.

Honey was the first form of sweetener known. Sugar did not come into widespread use until the Middle Ages, although at that time it was still considered a luxury and was very expensive. During the seventeenth century sugar became readily available. It came to Europe from North Africa, where the Crusaders first encountered it during their journeys to the Holy Land. Venice was the center of trade for sugar during its height as a trading capital in the thirteenth century.

All sugar attracts moisture and can become lumpy during storage, so it is best to store sugar in as airtight a container as possible.

Granulated Sugar. Granulated sugar, also called sucrose, is the most common form of sugar. Processed from sugarcane, it is a complex or double sugar composed of both fructose and glucose, which are simple sugars. When sugar is called for in the recipes in this book, use granulated sugar unless otherwise specified.

Confectioners' Sugar. This is made from very finely ground granulated sugar with a small amount of cornstarch added to prevent caking. Confectioners' sugar always has to be sifted before use. The main use for confectioners' sugar is for decorating and finishing.

Brown Sugar. Brown sugar has molasses added to liquid sucrose during processing. It is very rich and flavorful. Light brown sugar is used in the recipes in this book. Dark brown sugar has a very pronounced flavor. Brown sugar will dry out and become very hard if exposed to the air. It is always measured by packing it tightly.

Corn Syrup. Refined from cornstarch with water added, corn syrup comes in both light and dark forms. Light corn syrup is more highly refined; dark corn syrup contains molasses and has a robust flavor. The recipes in this book specify which type should be used. They are not interchangeable, due to the different flavors they impart. Both light and dark corn syrup add sweetness and moistness, and act as an interfering agent to prevent sugar from crystallizing and becoming grainy during cooking.

Honey. Honey is a natural sweetener. Its flavor varies depending on the area where it is produced and the type of flowers that the bees have fed upon. It has a distinct flavor and should be added to recipes only when its flavor is desired. Honey attracts moisture and, therefore, helps keep candies moist. Adding honey to sugar as it is cooking helps to prevent the sugar from crystallizing.

Maple Syrup. This highly valued natural sweetener comes from the sap of maple trees, which is boiled to remove the impurities. The higher grades are lighter and more delicate in flavor, and more desirable for use in candymaking. Be sure to use only pure maple syrup, not maple-flavored syrup. Maple syrup should be stored in the refrigerator after it has been opened.

Vanilla Beans

Native to Mexico, vanilla beans are the fruit of a climbing orchid. The plants are widely grown in tropical climates, such as Tahiti and Madagascar, which produce the most moist and flavorful vanilla beans. Vanilla beans impart an incomparable flavor to truffles, candies, and confections. Vanilla beans will dry out if left exposed to air, so they should be stored tightly covered in a dry, cool place. To flavor candies, the bean is split open and steeped in liquid. The tiny black grains that fill the inside of the bean contain the essential vanilla flavor, which is released when the bean is steeped. After using a vanilla bean, rinse and dry it, then bury it in your sugar canister, where it will continue to impart its characteristic perfume to the sugar. The best vanilla beans can be purchased from cookware shops or stores that specialize in spices. The vanilla beans found in supermarkets are usually old and dried out.

Equipment & Tools

*M*aking the recipes in this book is meant to be easy and fun. By using the correct equipment and tools, you will obtain the best results, in the least amount of time and with the least amount of effort. For example, using a large chef's knife to chop block chocolate is much easier and faster than trying to use a paring knife.

Good-quality equipment and tools are an investment that will last for many years. Because inferior equipment and tools have to be replaced regularly, in the long run the best can cost you less. Many items in my kitchen have been with me for several years and, I am sure, have many more years of use.

The following list explains the most often used equipment and tools for the recipes in this book. All of the items are available in cookware shops, candymaking supply stores, the housewares section of department stores, major supermarkets, and from mail-order sources. Before beginning a recipe, check to see if you have everything you need. Many of these items are found in most home kitchens.

Candy / Sugar Thermometer

A necessity for accuracy in making candies and confections is a mercury thermometer designed specifically for candymaking and sugar work that reads in two-degree gradations in the range of 100° to 400°F. Erring a few degrees in either direction can spell disaster in cooked sugar syrups and candy mixtures, so be sure to buy a good-quality thermometer. To check a thermometer for accuracy, place it in a pan of water and bring the water to a boil. If the thermometer reads 212°F, it is correct. If it reads a degree or two above or below 212°F, take note that the thermometer is off by that amount and adjust the temperatures in the recipes accordingly. The sugar thermometer I like to use is made by Taylor. It has a metal frame that holds the mercury-filled glass case. This frame touches the bottom of the pan and suspends the bulb of the thermometer in the mixture, allowing an accurate reading. If using another type of thermometer, make sure to hold it so that the bulb is suspended in the mixture, otherwise you will be taking the temperature of the bottom of the pan.

Make sure to read the thermometer at eye level for accuracy. Treat your thermometer with care. Do not take a thermometer from a hot liquid and plunge it into cold water. Place it in hot water or allow it to cool on a countertop. Store the thermometer where it will not be jostled by other utensils, which can cause the mercury to separate or the glass to crack (see page 16, on chocolate thermometers.)

Candy and Truffle Dippers

These European hand tools are designed to hold truffles and candies for dipping into chocolate. There are oval shapes, round shapes, spiral shapes, and several different types of dipping forks. These dippers are made of a 3-inch-long round, thin metal strip with the shape at the top end. The metal strip is attached to a 3 1/2-inch-long wooden handle. There are also domestically made plastic dipping tools that work well for dipping truffles and candies.

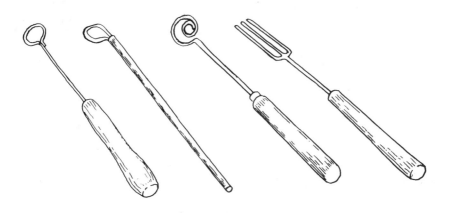

Chef's Knife

A knife with an 8-inch or 10-inch blade is very handy for chopping block chocolate in small pieces, chopping nuts, cutting dried fruit, and cutting brittles, caramels, and nougats. Keep the blade sharp and store the knife in a block or a knife rack.

Chocolate Mold

Transparent plastic chocolate molds of many different shapes and sizes are available in cookware shops and shops that sell candymaking supplies. Make sure that the cavities of the molds are not scratched, which will make the molded chocolate difficult to remove. Wash chocolate molds in warm, soapy water and dry them with a soft towel. Do not use abrasive cleaners or cleaning pads, which will scratch the molds. Store the molds in a cool, dry place. Make sure that they are completely dry before using them for molding.

Chocolate Thermometer

Glass mercury thermometers that read in one-degree gradations in the range of 40° to 130°F have been created specifically for chocolate. They are designed and manufactured to be extremely accurate, which is a necessity in working with chocolate. Being off by as little as 1 or 2 degrees can make an enormous difference in chocolate work. A chocolate thermometer should be handled with extreme care. When it is removed from a warm pan of chocolate, the bulb should be wiped off immediately with paper towels. As with a candy thermometer, store this thermometer where it will not be jostled by other utensils, which can cause the mercury to separate or the glass to crack. I keep two chocolate thermometers on hand as a precaution.

Copper Sugar Pan

Unlined copper pans, with straight sides and a pour spout, are designed especially for cooking sugar. These pans are also called caramel pans, because they are often used for cooking sugar to caramel. Copper is the best material for conducting heat evenly and consistently. Copper stands up extremely well to the high temperatures needed for cooking sugar mixtures. It is easy to see the changes in color when cooking sugar in a copper pan because of the light background color of the pan. The easiest way to remove sugar that sticks to the pan is to fill the pan with water and bring it to a boil. To clean copper use a solution of salt and vinegar or lemon juice. Rub this all over the pan vigorously, rinse off, and dry the pan with a soft towel.

Double Boiler

A double boiler is necessary for melting chocolate. Make sure that the top pan fits tightly over the bottom pan so no water or steam can escape and mix with the chocolate. I often use a glass double boiler, which allows me to see the water in the bottom pan. I also make my own double boilers with a 3-quart saucepan for the bottom and a 2-quart stainless steel mixing bowl for the top pan. The bowl fits snugly over the bottom pan. This allows me to use the same bottom pan for melting many bowls of chocolate. Avoid using a small double boiler for melting a large quantity of chocolate. It will take too long to melt the chocolate and it will be difficult to stir the chocolate if the pan is too small.

Electric Mixer

A stand-up mixer is the easiest and most convenient type of mixer to use for candymaking. It allows you to have your hands free for other tasks. A hand-held mixer will work, though it will just take a few minutes longer. I use a Kitchenaid K5SS with a 5-quart capacity, which is the same design as the commercial mixers but on a smaller scale. Many people prefer the smaller K45SS with the head that tips back. It is purely a matter of preference.

Flan Ring

Also called a flan form, this 1-inch-high metal form has no top or bottom. It is used for shaping candies. A flan ring is always placed on a baking sheet lined with aluminum foil, parchment, or waxed paper, which becomes the bottom of the form. Flan rings come in many shapes and sizes—rectangular, round, square, and daisy petal.

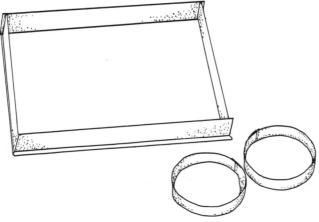

Flexible-Blade Spatula

The stainless steel blade of this spatula has rounded ends and straight sides and is set into a wooden handle. The blade should be flexible but not spongy. The spatulas are available in many blade sizes. For candymaking I use those with a narrow 4-inch blade and 6-inch blade.

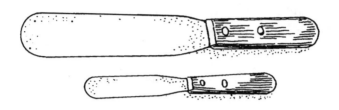

Foil Candy Cup

Fluted-edge candy cups made of colored foil are 1 inch in diameter and 5/8 inch deep. They come in a box of 40 or 60 in three different colors: red, green, and gold. They are very sturdy, which makes them perfect for holding truffle creams and candy mixtures that are still liquid. When they are peeled away from a candy, they leave their attractive fluted design around the sides.

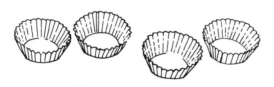

Heavy-Bottomed Saucepan

These saucepans protect the mixtures they hold from too much heat as they cook. Most candy mixtures are cooked to high temperatures over a period of time. If a thin saucepan is used, it will almost unfailingly scorch the mixture. I use Le Creuset enameled cast iron pans and occasionally Calphalon, which is made of heavy anodized aluminum. Both are excellent heat conductors and are heavy enough to keep prolonged heat from burning their mixtures.

Offset Spatula

This stainless steel spatula has a flexible blade attached to a wooden handle. The tip of the blade is round and blunt. The body of the blade has straight sides. The blade has a bend or angle near the handle that is stepped down approximately 1 inch from the handle. Two sizes are most useful for candymaking: a 12-inch blade for spreading chocolate for tempering and a 4-inch blade for small work and decorating.

Marble Board

Marble is the ideal material for cooling hot mixtures because it maintains a consistently cooler temperature than other materials and dissipates the heat quickly. It is invaluable in candy work. Marble is used for tempering chocolate, rolling and cooling brittles, and cooling fudge. Marble is heavy, so buy a piece that is not too large to move, since it needs to be cleaned after use. I have a marble board that is 18 inches by 24 inches by 3/4 inch. It always sits on my countertop, so it is ready to use. Don't use your marble for a cutting board. Not only will it rapidly dull your knives, but cuts will interfere with your chocolate and candy work.

Measuring Cups

It is important to use different measuring cups for liquid and dry ingredients. Dry measures come in a graduated set; they nest together, are flat on top, and have long handles. Sizes usually available are 1/8 cup, 1/4 cup, 1/3 cup, 1/2 cup, and 1 cup. These are designed to be filled and leveled off. To measure dry ingredients, such as sugar, scoop the sugar into the measure, then use a knife to sweep off the excess so that the top of the measure is flat.

Glass or plastic measuring cups with a pour spout are for liquid ingredients and should be read at eye level. These are designed to have extra room at the top so liquids won't spill as they are being moved. These measures should not be used for measuring dry ingredients, since there is no way to level them at the top. I keep 2 sets of dry measures in a drawer with my measuring spoons.

Measuring Spoons

A graduated set of measuring spoons is essential for measuring ingredients accurately. Measuring spoons come in the standard sizes of 1/4 teaspoon, 1/2 teaspoon, 1 teaspoon, and 1 tablespoon. They are used for both dry and liquid ingredients. For dry ingredients, scoop the spoon into the ingredient and level it off with a knife or spatula. For liquid ingredients, pour the ingredient carefully into the spoon so that it doesn't spill. Two sets of measuring spoons will save time, since you won't have to wash them as you are working on a recipe.

Paper Candy Cup

Fluted-edge candy cups made of paper are 1 1/2 inches in diameter and 5/8 inch high. They are sometimes called petit-four cases. Paper candy cups are inexpensive, so it is a good idea to keep a stock in your cupboard. They are made of thin paper and are designed to hold finished truffles and candies. Professional confectioners use glassine cups, which do not absorb the oil from candies. Paper candy cups come in different colors, but brown is the most often used. For Valentine's Day and the Christmas holiday season I like to use red paper candy cups.

Paper Pastry Cone

Made from a triangle of parchment paper, either bought precut or cut yourself, this cone is used for decorating and for filling chocolate molds. Make up several of them and keep them in your cupboard so they will be ready for you to use. See page 35 for diagram.

Parchment Paper

Nonstick parchment paper has many uses in candymaking: for making paper pastry cones, for measuring onto and holding dry ingredients, and for lining baking sheets to hold finished candies, among others. It comes in rolls in boxes that look like aluminum foil boxes or in large sheets that can be cut to the size needed.

Pastry Bag and Tip

Most truffle mixtures need to be shaped with a pastry bag and tip. Soft polyester or nylon pastry bags that can be washed are the best. I find the 12-inch and 14-inch pastry bags the most useful sizes. They can hold a sufficient supply of a mixture without overfilling them, so they are easy to handle. It is best to fill a pastry bag no more than halfway for ease of handling. When you buy a new pastry bag, it is necessary to cut off about 1/2 inch at the end for the pastry tip to fit through. Try not to cut off too much or the tip will fall out of the bag. Disposable plastic bags are also available, but I find that if much pressure is exerted on them while piping, they split. Launder pastry bags inside out in hot, soapy water, then stand them wide end down on a countertop to dry. Pastry bags also can be washed in the dishwasher or the washing machine.

I always use large 2-inch-high pastry tips, not the small ones that are used for cake decorating. Ateco and Magic Line make very good quality, accurate tips. Numbers 4, 5, and 6 are the sizes I use the most for candymaking. These are plain round tips with a 1/2-inch (approximately) opening. All pastry tips have their number, which indicates the size, etched on the front.

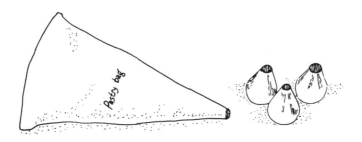

Pastry Brush

The best candymaking brushes are natural bristle, not nylon, and are flat, 1 inch wide, with a wooden handle. I keep separate the brushes that I use for washing down the sides of the pan while sugar is cooking. That way I'm sure that no grease or other material has tainted them. Wash pastry brushes in hot, soapy water, rinse, squeeze out the excess water, and air dry. About once a month I wash my pastry brushes in the dishwasher. This is not the best treatment for the wooden handles, but it thoroughly cleans the bristles.

Pastry Comb

Made of either metal or plastic with serrated edges similar to saw teeth, a pastry comb is used for decorating. Metal pastry combs are usually 4 inches wide and small enough to be held in your palm, or they can be triangular in shape. Plastic pastry combs look like a long 1-inch-wide ruler. Both types have different-sized teeth on each edge.

Pastry Scraper / Bench Scraper

Plastic pastry scrapers are very useful when hand tempering chocolate. They are about 4 1/2 inches wide, 3 1/2 inches high, and fit into your hand. They also work very well for scraping out mixing bowls.

Bench scrapers are made of stainless steel and have a wooden handle. The blade is wide and flat with sharp edges, and measures 6 inches by 3 inches. This tool also fits into your hand. It is most useful for cleaning and scraping surfaces, such as removing hardened chocolate or brittles from marble.

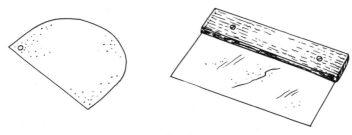

Rolling Pin

A heavy rolling pin is necessary to roll out brittles and toffee. The best materials are marble, steel, or copper, although wooden rolling pins work well. I use a copper-covered wooden rolling pin for candy work. Make sure that the rolling pin is heavy enough so that it does most of the work for you. Also make sure that it is large enough so you can easily and rapidly roll out a hot mixture without burning your hands.

Rubber Spatula

A rubber spatula doesn't absorb other flavors, so it is superior to wooden spoons for stirring chocolate. Be sure to use a brand that is flexible and has a rubber handle.

I use Rubbermaid rubber spatulas in two sizes. The smaller size is 9 1/4 inches in length, with the blade measuring 3 1/4 inches by 2 inches. The larger size is 13 1/2 inches long with a blade measuring 4 1/2 inches by 2 3/4 inches. Both blades are curved on one side of the top. This makes it easy to get into corners and small spaces. Both sizes are also very useful for scraping out mixing bowls. Good-quality rubber spatulas can be washed in the dishwasher and will last for many years.

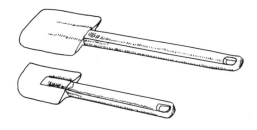

Scale

If you are buying chocolate in bulk and chopping it yourself, an accurate kitchen scale is necessary to measure it, since it is not marked into ounces. Whether you use a balance scale or a spring scale, be sure that it is accurate. A good test for accuracy is to weigh a pound of butter. I use a Soehnle kitchen scale that has a dial I can adjust to zero each time I weigh an item. It also holds different-sized bowls on top, so I can weigh in the same bowl I am using for the top of my double boiler.

Storage Container

Plastic storage containers are very useful for storing nuts, dried fruits, and other raw ingredients. Truffles, candies, and confections must be stored in tightly covered containers for maximum freshness. I use plastic containers with lids that seal snugly, such as Tupperware. I also use tins that I line with aluminum foil or waxed paper. Whatever you use, make sure that it seals tightly and the material it is made from will not interfere with the flavor of the contents. For holiday gift giving I use attractive tins. I am always on the search for charming and unusual tins to use for this purpose.

Strainer

Plastic mesh strainers are the best since the plastic will not react with any of the ingredients. Also, they can be washed in the dishwasher. The most useful sizes for straining liquids, pureeing fruits, and sifting cocoa powder and confectioners' sugar are the round-bottomed, 4-inch diameter and 6-inch diameter fine mesh strainers.

Sugar Dredger

A dredger looks like a large salt shaker (about 2 1/2 inches in diameter) with a handle and an arched mesh screen on top. Using a dredger is the best way to dust your hands and the tops of truffles with confectioners' sugar or cocoa powder. A dredger allows you to have control over how much confectioners' sugar or cocoa powder you use. I use plastic dredgers so they can be washed in the dishwasher as needed. I keep two dredgers, one for confectioners' sugar and one for cocoa powder.

Tempering Machine

Professional confectioners and chocolatiers use tempering machines, which melt chocolate slowly, temper the chocolate, and hold it at the correct temperature for dipping candies and truffles. Tempering machines come in many different sizes and capacities with small machines for home use. A tempering machine is an expensive item and there are just a few on the market to choose from. The two most popular ones are American Chocolate Mould Company's Table Top Temperer and Hilliard's Little Dipper.

A tempering machine is very easy to use. Simply turn on the machine, put in the chopped-up chocolate, and set the temperature dial according to the instructions. Allow some time for tempering chocolate with a machine. It takes approximately an hour. Perfect results are guaranteed with a tempering machine. One very nice feature of the machine is that you can hold the chocolate at a constant temperature to keep it liquid overnight, then in the morning adjust the temperature to temper the chocolate. This way the chocolate can be tempered faster than starting with newly chopped chocolate. A couple of tips that are worth mentioning: clean up of a tempering machine is a big job; however, the bowls lift out for cleaning. Also, take care that the chopped chocolate doesn't build up behind the scraper and push itself up over the edge of the bowl.

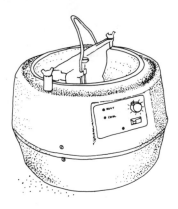

Wooden Spoon and Spatula

These are invaluable for stirring hot candy mixtures, such as brittles, caramels, fudges, and nougats. Since wood doesn't conduct heat, the utensils will stay cool. Also, they won't scratch the bottom of your pans. The long-handled type is best so you can keep your hands a good distance from the hot mixture. Wooden spatulas that have a straight edge are very handy for stirring mixtures cooked over high heat. The flat edge covers more of the bottom of the pan than a rounded spoon. Wooden spoons and spatulas should not soak in water or be washed in the dishwasher, which will cause them to splinter and deteriorate over time.

Zester

This specially designed tool removes the aromatic outer rind of citrus fruits in thin strips, without also removing the inner white pith, which is bitter. It has five small sharp holes at the end of a strip of metal attached to a handle, which is usually plastic or wood. Make sure to buy a zester that has sharp holes. It is frustrating to zest a lemon or orange with a dull zester.

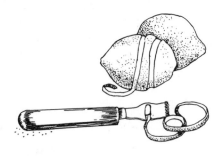

Techniques

$\mathcal{N}$ ot enough can be said about the importance of using the correct techniques when making truffles, candies, and confections. Like using the best ingredients and equipment, using the correct techniques ensures the most delicious and beautiful results. Also, using the correct techniques will help you to spend less time in the kitchen and more time enjoying the fruits of your labor.

Working With Chocolate

Handling Chocolate. Chocolate needs to be handled with care. Water, or any liquid, is the enemy of chocolate. A few drops of liquid can cause a pan of chocolate to "seize up," to the point where its texture resembles mud. If this happens, there is nothing you can do to salvage it. Some people add vegetable oil to their seized chocolate; however, it no longer tastes like chocolate, and it cannot be used as pure chocolate. Prevent any moisture from coming in contact with chocolate unless it is specifically called for in a recipe. Make sure that all utensils used with chocolate are completely dry.

The ideal environment for working with chocolate is 65°F and low humidity. Needless to say, foggy and rainy days are not good for chocolate work. Neither are summer days of 80°F or more. Air-conditioning helps when it's very hot, as does a humidifier when it's very humid.

Melting Chocolate. To melt chocolate it should be cut or chopped into very small pieces and placed in the top of a double boiler over hot, not simmering, water. Make sure that the top of the double boiler fits tightly over the bottom pan, so that water cannot enter the top pan. Chocolate should be melted slowly and should not be heated over 120°F (110°F for white chocolate), which is slightly more than lukewarm. If the water becomes hotter than this, the chocolate will burn. Burned chocolate, like burned anything, does not taste good. Also, overheating chocolate can cause it to become grainy and to seize.

Use a plastic or rubber spatula to stir the chocolate frequently as it is melting. Wooden utensils are porous and hold the flavors of food, whereas plastic does not. Many people advocate melting chocolate in a microwave oven. I do not. It is much too easy to burn chocolate this way.

When the top pan of the double boiler is removed from the water, be sure to wipe the bottom of it very dry. Even a stray drop or two of water running down the side of the pan as the chocolate is being poured into another container is enough to seize the chocolate.

Tempering Chocolate. Tempering is the process that controls the crystalline structure of the unstable cocoa butter molecule, which has several different melting points, and sets this molecule at its most stable point. Tempering gives chocolate a shiny, unblemished appearance and smooth texture. All chocolate comes from the factory tempered. When chocolate is melted, it goes out of temper and must be tempered again before it is used for dipping and molding. Untempered, or out of temper, chocolate has an unsightly appearance and grainy texture. Gray or white streaks and dots appear on the surface. This is known as "chocolate bloom." Tempered chocolate sets up rapidly, has a clean, sharp snap when it breaks, and releases easily from molds because it shrinks as it cools.

To temper chocolate it needs to be heated, cooled, and heated again, which stabilizes the cocoa butter crystals. There are several methods for tempering chocolate. The classic method produces the best and most reliable results. The quick tempering method also will bring good results, but the chocolate will be less stable and go out of temper faster. For this reason, I recommend using the classic method. Both the classic and quick methods are described here. Another method of tempering chocolate is to use a tempering machine (see page 24), which produces excellent results. Simply follow the manufacturer's directions to use the machine.

Classic Method for Tempering Chocolate

Chop 1 pound of chocolate into small pieces and place them in the top of a double boiler over hot, not simmering, water, stirring frequently with a rubber spatula to ensure even melting. Remove the double boiler from the heat, then remove the top pan from the double boiler and wipe it dry. Stir the chocolate several times to begin cooling it. Pour about two thirds of the chocolate onto a marble board. With an offset spatula spread the chocolate out into a large rectangle, then with a plastic pastry scraper gather it back into a pool in the center of the marble. Repeat this process three or four times, then take the temperature of the chocolate with a chocolate thermometer. It should be between 78° and 80°F.

Scrape the pool of chocolate back into the pan with the remaining third and stir together gently until thoroughly blended (2 to 3 minutes). The final temperature for the tempered chocolate should be 88° to 91°F for dark chocolate, 85° to 88°F for milk chocolate, and 84° to 87°F for white chocolate.

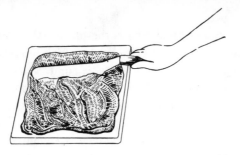

With an offset spatula spread the chocolate out into a large rectangle on a marble plate.

Use a plastic pastry scraper to gather it back into a pool in the center of the marble. Repeat this process three or four times.

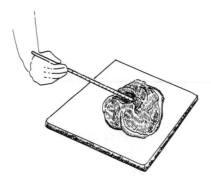

Take the temperature of the chocolate with a chocolate thermometer. It should be between 78° and 80°F.

If the temperature of the finished chocolate is slightly lower than it should be, warm the chocolate in the double boiler over low heat just until it reaches the correct temperature. If the temperature of the chocolate is higher than it should be, the tempering process must be repeated to bring the chocolate to its correct point.

Once the chocolate is tempered, it needs to be held at the same temperature while you dip the truffles and candies. To do this, place the pan of tempered chocolate over a pan of water that is 2° warmer than the chocolate. Change this water periodically to keep it at the correct temperature. Another method for maintaining the temperature of the tempered chocolate is to place the pan of tempered chocolate on a heating pad set at its lowest temperature.

Be sure to stir the chocolate occasionally as you are using it. Chocolate that builds up around the sides of the pan will begin to cool and go out of temper if it is not stirred back into the pan. If you are dipping truffles and candies over a long period of time, it may be necessary to temper the chocolate again if it becomes too cool.

Quick Tempering Method for Chocolate

Chop 1 pound of chocolate into very small pieces and set aside one third of them. Melt the remaining two thirds in the top of a double boiler over hot, not simmering, water, stirring frequently with a rubber spatula to ensure even melting. The chocolate should not exceed 120°F (110°F for white chocolate) or it will burn. Remove the double boiler from the heat, then remove the top pan of the double boiler and wipe it dry. Stir in the remaining chocolate in three batches, making sure that each batch is completely melted before adding the next. When all the chocolate has been added, the chocolate will be tempered.

Molding Chocolate. Solid molding requires tempered chocolate. Transfer the tempered chocolate to a large parchment paper pastry cone (see page 35), fold down the top edges of the pastry cone securely, then cut off a 1/4-inch-wide opening at the pointed tip of the cone. Squeeze chocolate into each cavity of the mold just up to the top edge. With a small flexible blade spatula clean off the edges of the cavities. Tap the mold on a countertop a few times to eliminate air pockets. Place the mold on a flat surface in the freezer for 15 minutes. Remove the mold and turn it upside down over a piece of parchment or waxed paper. Hold the mold by opposite corners and gently twist it in opposite directions. The chocolates should drop out of the mold. If they don't drop out easily, return the mold to the freezer for another 15 minutes, and try again.

An easy way to tell if the chocolate will release from the mold is to hold the mold flat above your head. Look at the cavities of the mold from this viewpoint. If the cavities are completely clear, the chocolate has shrunk away from the mold and will release easily. If the chocolate is visible and frosty-looking, then the mold needs to chill several more minutes before the chocolate will release easily.

A hollow mold has a thin outer shell of chocolate that can be filled with a truffle cream or other liquid mixture. Follow the above directions for solid molding up to the point where the mold is filled with chocolate and tapped on the countertop to eliminate air pockets, then let the chocolate sit in the mold for 3 minutes at room temperature. Turn the mold upside down over a piece of parchment or waxed paper and let the excess chocolate run out. The mold is now coated with a thin outer shell of chocolate and ready for its filling. Quickly clean off the edges of each cavity, if necessary. The filling should be inserted immediately, filling each cavity of the mold three quarters full. Pipe tempered chocolate over the filling just up to the top edge of each cavity to "cap off" the mold. Chill the mold in the freezer and unmold following the above instructions for solid molding.

Kneading Marzipan

Kneading is a process of mixing and working a substance until it is smooth and supple. Flavors and colors are blended into marzipan most successfully by hand kneading. To add flavor to marzipan, make a well in the center of the marzipan and add the flavor (usually a teaspoon of liqueur or extract). To add color to marzipan use a toothpick with a few drops of paste food color and insert the toothpick into the marzipan in several places. To knead marzipan gather it into a ball on a smooth work surface. Push the marzipan away from yourself with the heel of your hand while pressing down into it, then gather it back into a ball, folding it over itself. Give the marzipan a one-quarter turn, then repeat this process several times until a smooth texture is reached and the flavor and color are thoroughly blended (10 to 15 minutes).

Working With Nuts

Toasting Nuts. Toasting enhances the flavor of nuts. To toast nuts, spread them in a single layer on an ungreased baking sheet and place them in a 350°F preheated oven. For almonds and most other nuts, stir them in the pan every 5 minutes and toast until light golden colored (about 15 minutes), then remove the baking sheet from the oven and let it cool on a rack. For hazelnuts toast them until the skins begin to split and the nuts are light golden colored (15 to 18 minutes). Remove the baking sheet from the oven, let the hazelnuts sit for 10 minutes, then rub the hazelnuts between your hands to help remove the skins. Not all the skins will release from all the hazelnuts, so separate out those that are totally skinned and save them for decorating.

Grinding Nuts. When nuts are ground they release their natural oils. To absorb this oil and prevent the nuts from becoming pasty while grinding, I add a small amount of sugar. For each cup of nuts, except for hazelnuts, add 1 tablespoon of sugar. For each cup of hazelnuts add 2 tablespoons of sugar.

Chopping Nuts. Nuts can be chopped by hand with a large (10-inch blade) chef's knife on a cutting board, or in a food processor fitted with a steel blade. With the food processor use a pulsing action for 30 seconds to 1 minute, depending on how fine the nuts need to be chopped.

Blanching Nuts. To blanch nuts drop them into a pan of boiling water and leave them for 1 minute. Remove the nuts from the pan with a skimmer or slotted spoon and place them in a bowl of cold water. The skins should release easily as you squeeze each nut. If the skins do not release easily, return the nuts to the boiling water for another 30 seconds and try again.

Measuring Dry Ingredients

Use dry measuring cups that can be swept off at the top, not the liquid measures with pour spouts. I use the scoop and sweep method. Scoop the measure into the ingredient, or spoon the ingredient into the measure, heaping it slightly over the top. With the flat edge of a knife or spatula, sweep off the excess, leveling the top.

Packing Candies and Confections for Gifts and to Mail

Attractive tins provide the best protection for your confections that need to travel through the mail. They also make an appealing presentation for your confections given as gifts. Pack the confections in the tins in single layers between sheets of waxed paper. For extra protection wrap the tins in aluminum foil and mail them in padded envelopes. It's helpful to include a note telling the recipient either to eat the confections promptly, or store them in the refrigerator and then bring them to room temperature before serving.

Pastry Bag Techniques

Preparing a Pastry Bag. It is necessary to cut off about a 1/2 inch at the pointed end of a new pastry bag for the tube to fit through. Drop the tube into the bag, thin end down. Mark the line to be cut with a pencil, remove the tube from the bag, and use sharp scissors to cut the pastry bag. Reinsert the tube into the pastry bag. If the cut has been made correctly, the end of the tube will show out of the end of the pastry bag. Do not cut off too much of the pastry bag, or the tube may fall out.

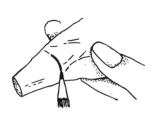  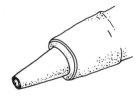

Filling and Refilling the Pastry Bag. Fold down the top edge of the pastry bag a generous 2 to 3 inches to form a cuff. Hold the pastry bag underneath the cuff or hold the pastry bag upright in a jar or measuring cup. Use a rubber spatula to fill the bag not more than halfway for ease of handling. Unfold the cuff over the filling. Holding the pastry bag by the top end, push the filling down toward the tip. Twist the pastry bag tightly at the point where the filling ends, and hold the pastry bag between your thumb and forefinger to secure the filling. Squeeze a small amount of the filling back into the bowl to release any air caught in the bag. To refill the bag, fold the cuff down and repeat the above process.

Piping With the Pastry Bag. The pressure to squeeze out the filling from the pastry bag is applied with the palm and fingers of the hand holding the bag. The fingers of the other hand are used to help guide the pastry bag, and rest gently above the tube. To pipe truffles and fill molds with a pastry bag, hold the pastry bag with the end of the tube perpendicular to and 1 inch above the piping surface. Squeeze out a small mound of the mixture, maintaining even pressure on the pastry bag, then release the pressure and pull the pastry bag away from the mound.

Paper Pastry Cones

Making a Paper Pastry Cone. Cut or use a parchment paper triangle measuring 12 inches by 12 inches by 15 inches. Hold the triangle in front of you with the point facing down. Take the right corner and curve it in, bringing the point down to meet the bottom point. Hold the two ends together with your left hand (or right hand if you are left-handed). With your right hand, wrap the left point of the triangle around the outside and bring the point down to meet the other points, forming a cone. Make sure that the pointed end of the cone is not open. Place a piece of tape over the outside back seam of the cone, then fold the top edges in twice, making an even top edge.

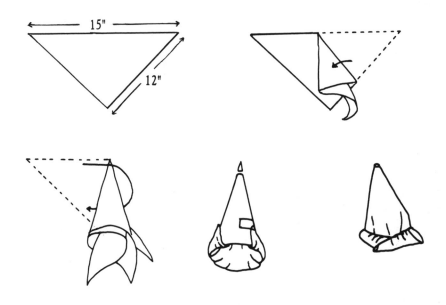

Using and Piping With a Paper Pastry Cone. To fill the paper pastry cone, hold the cone near the pointed end and use a rubber spatula to place the filling into the pastry cone, filling it no more than halfway. Fold in each side of the top of the pastry cone to the center, then roll the top down until it meets the filling. The pastry cone must be tightly closed to prevent the filling from coming out the top. With sharp scissors cut off a small (1/4-inch to 1/2-inch) opening at the pointed end. Hold the pastry cone between your thumb and fingers and use the pressure from your fingers to push the mixture from the cone. Use the fingers of your other hand to help guide the pastry cone, resting your fingers slightly above the pointed end of the cone. Hold the paper pastry cone perpendicular to and 1 inch above the piping surface. Squeeze gently and evenly on the pastry cone to allow the mixture to flow out. To stop the mixture from flowing, release the pressure on the pastry cone and pull the cone away.

Fill the pastry cone no more than halfway.

Tightly close pastry cone and cut off a small (1/4-inch to 1/2-inch) opening at the pointed end.

Squeeze gently and evenly on the pastry cone to allow the mixture to flow out.

Using a Zester

To zest a lemon, a lime, or an orange, hold the stem ends of the fruit between your thumb and fingers, then place the zester's sharp-holed end against the top edge of the fruit. Lightly push the zester so that it will cut into the colored part of the rind, then pull the zester from the top end of the fruit to the bottom. This removes long strands of the rind. Repeat this motion all around the fruit, which removes all the outer rind. Make sure not to go over an area that has already been zested or you will remove the white part, or pith, which is bitter. After removing all the zest use a sharp chef's knife to dice the zest finely. See page 25.

Do-Ahead Tips for Making an Assortment of
Truffles, Candies and Confections

An assortment of candies given as a gift, set out on a buffet table, or served after a dinner party is always appreciated. In order to make an assortment of candies, some advance planning and organization is necessary. Here are some tips to help you.

1. Decide which truffles, candies, and confections you want to include in your assortment. Four to six candies makes an appealing presentation. Be sure to check the yield for each recipe, so that you prepare the amount of candy you need.

2. Carefully read through each of the recipes you have chosen to be sure you understand what ingredients, equipment, tools, and techniques are needed for preparation.

3. Make your shopping list, then purchase the necessary ingredients and anything else you may need.

4. Make a list of the various tasks that need to be done in order to make the candies you have chosen. Number the tasks in the order in which they need to be accomplished. Tasks that can be done well in advance should be placed at the top of the list, and last-minute tasks placed at the bottom. For example, preparing truffle creams would be placed at the top of the list because they can be made and kept in the refrigerator for a few weeks. Be sure to cross each task off of the list as it is completed.

5. Do as much preparation in advance as possible. Measuring ingredients, chopping and portioning chocolate, making truffle creams, and blanching, toasting, grinding, and chopping nuts are all tasks that can be accomplished in advance. In addition, truffles can be piped out, shaped, and rolled in advance, and brittles can be made and kept in airtight containers before they are dipped in chocolate. When I am going to prepare an assortment of truffles, candies, and confections, I spend a day doing preparation tasks such as chopping and portioning chocolate, preparing nuts, and making candied orange peel. For each recipe it is a good idea to measure out the necessary ingredients and set them on a tray.

6. If you plan to give your candies as gifts, make up your gift packages a day or two before giving or sending them. This will save you from having to assemble your

packages in a hurry. Keep each package well wrapped in the refrigerator until it is ready to be given or mailed. As mentioned earlier, many of the candies in this book can be kept in tightly covered and well-wrapped containers in the refrigerator for up to one month, or in the freezer for two months. Be sure to defrost them in the refrigerator for at least 24 hours if they have been frozen. Leave enough time to bring them to room temperature before serving.

7. Do not leave too many last-minute tasks. If you find yourself overwhelmed with things to do, stop and reorganize. You may want to complete the quicker recipes first and then go on to the recipes that require more tasks. Make sure you set aside time to make your truffles, candies, and confections and try not to get sidetracked with the telephone or other activities during your candymaking sessions.

Truffles

*T*ruffles are the ultimate chocolate delight. Rich and elegant confections that always satisfy, they have chocolate and cream centers surrounded by an outer coating of either tempered chocolate, cocoa powder, confectioners' sugar, shredded coconut, or finely chopped nuts. A good truffle is usually devoured in two bites and literally melts in your mouth.

Chocolate truffles share the same name as a fungi that grows around the roots of trees in France and Italy. Not just any fungi, these truffles are a highly treasured delicacy. Because classic chocolate truffles are generally made in a lopsided roundish shape about an inch in diameter—similar in shape to this fungi—and because they are also much sought after, the name *truffle* fits perfectly.

There are numerous variations of truffles. The basic truffle mixture can be enriched with butter and can be flavored with liqueurs, extracts, coffee, finely chopped nuts, fruit purees, or candied fruit. Also, a variety of ingredients can be combined to produce exciting flavors and tantalizing textures. These variations can greatly intensify the delight of eating chocolate.

Because many truffles are finished similarly, telling one from another can be confusing. Generally, a truffle's outer decoration is a clue to its identity.

Most important when making truffles is that only the very best quality ingredients be used. Because only a few ingredients are used to make truffles, the quality of these ingredients cannot be concealed. For the outer coating of truffles either regular chocolate or coverture (see page 7) can be used; just make sure that whichever is used is very good quality.

Truffles are about as close as you can come to eating pure chocolate. They go very well with after-dinner coffee, or afternoon tea, or as a snack. They are usually the centerpiece of an assortment of candies and almost invariably are eaten first. It is not easy to eat only one, but because they are so rich, even the most avid chocolate eater is satisfied fairly quickly.

Truffles are easy to make, and their preparation fits easily into today's busy lifestyle because there are stopping places where the truffles must rest and chill for several hours. Also, truffle cream can be made in advance and kept in the refrigerator for a few weeks, or it can be frozen for up to 4 months. If the truffle cream has been frozen, be sure to defrost it for at least 24 hours in the refrigerator before using.

When truffle cream has been chilled for a long time, it is necessary to let it stand at room temperature until it reaches the correct consistency before piping it out. If truffle cream is too cold, it will be too difficult to use. To assure the best results always read through each recipe before beginning.

Truffles store very well in the refrigerator. However, because chocolate is like a sponge, picking up other flavors easily, be careful where the truffles are placed in the refrigerator. Also, be sure to store the truffles in an airtight container and, for extra protection, wrap the container in several layers of aluminum foil.

Truffles can be frozen, but again, it is a good idea to cover the container with several layers of foil. If frozen, defrost the truffles for 24 hours in the refrigerator before bringing them to room temperature to serve, since rapid temperature changes cause the chocolate to develop streaks or spots, and could possibly cause the outer coating to crack. Truffles taste best when eaten at room temperature. If they are too cold, their glorious full flavor cannot develop and be fully appreciated.

Making truffles is a perfect social activity for family, friends, and children. Since truffles need to be hand rolled into balls, it's fun to have at least one extra pair of hands to help. Obviously, the rewards are great.

The recipes included in this chapter provide a wide range of choices for the truffle maker, and variations are offered with many of the recipes. Once you feel comfortable following the recipes, use your imagination to devise your own variations. I'm certain that making and eating the ultimate chocolate delight will be a satisfying and enjoyable experience.

Classic Chocolate Truffles

Yield: 60 1-inch round truffles

These truffles are as close as you can get to eating pure chocolate. When you bite through the outer coating, you are treated to a creamy rich chocolate center. They will make you feel like royalty.

Ingredients

1 pound bittersweet chocolate, finely chopped

1 1/2 cups whipping cream

3 to 4 tablespoons cocoa powder

1 1/2 pounds bittersweet chocolate, to be tempered (see pages 24, 29-31)

Melt the chopped chocolate in the top of a double boiler over hot, not simmering, water, stirring frequently with a rubber spatula to ensure even melting. In a 1-quart saucepan over medium heat, bring the cream to a boil. Remove both pans from the heat, remove the top pan from the double boiler and wipe it dry, pour the cream into the melted chocolate, and stir together until thoroughly blended. Transfer the mixture to a bowl, cover, let cool to room temperature, and chill in the refrigerator until thick but not stiff (2 to 3 hours).

Line 2 baking sheets with parchment or waxed paper. Fit a 12-inch pastry bag with a #5 large, plain round tip and fill partway with the truffle cream. Holding the pastry bag 1 inch above the paper, pipe out mounds about 1 inch in diameter. Cover the mounds with plastic wrap and chill in the freezer for 2 hours or in the refrigerator for 6 hours.

Dust your hands with cocoa powder and roll the mounds into balls. These will be the truffle centers. Cover and chill the centers for another 2 hours in the freezer.

Melt and temper the 1 1/2 pounds bittersweet chocolate. Line 2 more baking sheets with parchment or waxed paper. Remove the truffle centers from the freezer 1 sheet at a time. Place a truffle center into the tempered chocolate, coating it completely. With a dipper or fork remove the center from the chocolate, carefully shake off the excess chocolate, and turn the truffle out onto the paper. After dipping the truffles place 6 tablespoons of the tempered chocolate in a paper pastry cone and snip off a tiny opening at the end. Pipe several parallel lines across the tops of the truffles. Repeat with the remaining sheet of truffle centers.

Let the truffles set at room temperature or chill them in the refrigerator for 10 to 15 minutes. When the truffles are set, place them in paper candy cups. In a tightly covered container wrapped in several layers of aluminum foil, the truffles will keep for 1 month in the refrigerator or 2 months in the freezer. The truffles are best served at room temperature.

———— Variations ————

Instead of dipping the truffle centers into tempered chocolate, roll them in cocoa powder, confectioners' sugar, or finely chopped nuts as soon as they are rolled into balls.

Classic White Chocolate Truffles
Substitute 1 pound white chocolate for the bittersweet chocolate in the centers, and use 3/4 cup whipping cream. Dip the centers and line the tops of the truffles with tempered white chocolate, or roll the centers in confectioners' sugar as soon as they are rolled into balls.

Classic Milk Chocolate Truffles
Substitute milk chocolate for the bittersweet chocolate in the centers and for the coating, and use 1 cup whipping cream.

Swiss Chocolate Truffles

Yield: 60 1-inch round truffles

*These truffles follow the tradition of being dipped in chocolate twice.
The slight amount of Cognac used gives them an exquisite flavor.*

Ingredients

1 pound bittersweet chocolate, finely chopped

1 1/4 cups whipping cream

2 tablespoons unsalted butter, softened

2 tablespoons Cognac

3 to 4 tablespoons cocoa powder

2 pounds bittersweet chocolate, to be tempered (see pages 24, 29-31), divided

Melt the chopped chocolate in the top of a double boiler over hot, not simmering, water, stirring frequently with a rubber spatula to ensure even melting. In a 1-quart saucepan over medium heat, bring the cream to a boil. Remove both pans from the heat, remove the top pan from the double boiler and wipe it dry, pour the cream into the melted chocolate, and stir together until thoroughly blended. Add the butter and stir until it is melted, then blend in the Cognac. Transfer the mixture to a bowl, cover, let cool to room temperature, and chill in the refrigerator until thick but not stiff (2 to 3 hours).

Line 2 baking sheets with parchment or waxed paper. Fit a 12-inch pastry bag with a #5 large, plain round tip and fill partway with the truffle cream. Holding the pastry bag 1 inch above the paper, pipe out mounds about 1 inch in diameter. Cover the mounds with plastic wrap and chill in the freezer for 2 hours or in the refrigerator for 6 hours.

Dust your hands with cocoa powder and roll the mounds into balls. These will be the truffle centers. Cover and chill the centers for another 2 hours in the freezer.

Melt and temper 1 pound of the chocolate. Line 2 more baking sheets with parchment or waxed paper. Remove the truffle centers from the freezer 1 sheet at a time. Place a truffle center into the tempered chocolate, coating it completely. With a dipper or fork remove the center from the chocolate, carefully shake off the excess chocolate, and turn the truffle out onto the paper. Repeat with the remaining sheet of truffle centers.

Let the truffles set at room temperature or chill them in the refrigerator for 10 to 15 minutes. Line 2 more baking sheets with parchment or waxed paper. Melt and temper the remaining pound of chocolate and dip the truffles into the tempered chocolate, as above. Place the dipped truffles on the paper-lined baking sheets. After dipping 4 truffles, use the tines of a fork to lightly tap them all over to create a rough texture. When the truffles are set place them in paper candy cups. In a tightly covered container wrapped in several layers of aluminum foil, the truffles will keep for 1 month in the refrigerator or 2 months in the freezer. The truffles are best served at room temperature.

Variations

Swiss White Chocolate Truffles
Substitute white chocolate for the bittersweet chocolate in the centers and for the coating, and use 1/2 cup whipping cream.

Swiss Milk Chocolate Truffles
Substitute milk chocolate for the bittersweet chocolate in the centers and for the coating, and use 3/4 cup whipping cream.

Raspberry Chocolate Truffles

Yield: 60 1-inch round truffles

Raspberry and chocolate are a marvelous flavor combination. When you bite into one of these truffles, a burst of raspberry flavor is your reward.

Ingredients

1 cup fresh raspberries or 1 package (10 ounces) frozen raspberries, defrosted

4 tablespoons sugar

1 pound bittersweet chocolate, finely chopped

3/4 cup whipping cream

2 tablespoons corn syrup

2 tablespoons Framboise or Chambord

3/4 cup cocoa powder, divided

1 pound bittersweet chocolate, to be tempered (see pages 24, 29-31)

Purée the raspberries in a food processor or blender, then strain them to remove the seeds. Place the purée in a 1-quart heavy bottomed saucepan, add the sugar, and cook the mixture over medium heat until it is reduced by half (10 to 15 minutes), stirring frequently. Remove from the heat and let cool slightly.

Melt the chopped chocolate in the top of a double boiler over hot, not simmering, water, stirring frequently with a rubber spatula to ensure even melting. In a 1-quart saucepan over medium heat, bring the cream to a boil. Remove both pans from the heat, remove the top pan from the double boiler and wipe it dry, pour the cream into the chocolate, and stir together until thoroughly blended. Add the corn syrup, cooked raspberry purée, and liqueur, and blend thoroughly. Transfer the mixture to a bowl, cover, let cool to room temperature, and refrigerate until thick but not stiff (2 to 3 hours).

Line 2 baking sheets with parchment or waxed paper. Fit a 12-inch pastry bag with a #5 large, plain round tip and fill partway with the truffle cream. Holding the pastry bag 1 inch above the paper, pipe out mounds about 1 inch in diameter. Cover the mounds with plastic wrap and chill in the freezer for 2 hours or in the refrigerator for 6 hours.

Dust your hands with some of the cocoa powder and roll the mounds into balls. These will be the truffle centers. Cover and chill the centers for another 2 hours in the freezer.

Melt and temper the 1 pound bittersweet chocolate. Line 2 more baking sheets with parchment or waxed paper. Remove the truffle centers from the freezer 1 tray at a time. Place a truffle center into the tempered chocolate, coating it completely. With a dipper or fork remove the center from the chocolate, carefully shake off the excess chocolate, and turn the truffle out onto the paper. After dipping 6 truffles, dust the tops of them lightly with some of the remaining cocoa powder before the chocolate sets up. Repeat with the remaining sheet of truffle centers.

Let the truffles set at room temperature or chill them in the refrigerator for 10 to 15 minutes. When the truffles are set place them in paper candy cups. In a tightly covered container wrapped in several layers of aluminum foil, the truffles will keep for 1 month in the refrigerator or 2 months in the freezer. The truffles are best served at room temperature.

Hazelnut Chocolate Truffles

Yield: 60 1-inch round truffles

The finely ground hazelnuts in these truffles add extra depth to the flavor and a delightful crunch to the texture. Absolutely no one eats just one of these truffles.

Ingredients

1 pound bittersweet chocolate, finely chopped

1 1/2 cups whipping cream

1 cup toasted, skinned, and finely ground hazelnuts, divided

3 to 4 tablespoons cocoa powder

1 1/2 pounds bittersweet chocolate, to be tempered (see pages 24, 29-31)

Melt the chopped chocolate in the top of a double boiler over hot, not simmering, water, stirring frequently with a rubber spatula to ensure even melting. In a 1-quart saucepan over medium heat, bring the cream to a boil. Remove both pans from the heat, remove the top pan from the double boiler and wipe dry, pour the cream into the melted chocolate, and stir together until thoroughly blended. Mix in 3/4 cup of the hazelnuts and blend well. Transfer the mixture to a bowl, cover, let cool to room temperature, and chill in the refrigerator until thick but not stiff (2 to 3 hours).

Line 2 baking sheets with parchment or waxed paper. Fit a 12-inch pastry bag with a #5 large, plain round tip and fill partway with the truffle cream. Holding the pastry bag 1 inch above the paper, pipe out mounds about 1 inch in diameter. Cover the mounds with plastic wrap and chill in the freezer for 2 hours or in the refrigerator for 6 hours.

Dust your hands with cocoa powder and roll the mounds into balls. These will be the truffle centers. Cover and chill the centers for another 2 hours in the freezer.

Melt and temper the 1 1/2 pounds chocolate. Line 2 more baking sheets with parchment or waxed paper. Remove the truffle centers from the freezer 1 sheet at a time. Place a truffle center into the tempered chocolate, coating it completely. With a dipper or fork remove the center from the chocolate, carefully shake off the excess chocolate, and turn the truffle out onto the paper. After dipping 4 truffles, sprinkle a pinch of the remaining 1/4 cup ground hazelnuts on top of them, before the chocolate sets up completely. Repeat with the remaining sheet of truffle centers.

Let the truffles set at room temperature or chill them in the refrigerator for 10 to 15 minutes. When the truffles are set place them in paper candy cups. In a tightly covered container wrapped in several layers of aluminum foil, the truffles will keep for 1 month in the refrigerator or 2 months in the freezer. The truffles are best served at room temperature.

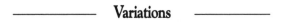

Variations

Instead of dipping the truffles in tempered chocolate, roll them in cocoa powder, confectioners' sugar, or finely chopped, toasted hazelnuts as soon as they are rolled into balls. Any nuts can be substituted for the hazelnuts both inside and outside of the truffles.

White Chocolate Hazelnut Truffles
Substitute white chocolate for the bittersweet chocolate in the centers and for the coating, and use 3/4 cup whipping cream.

Milk Chocolate Hazelnut Truffles
Substitute milk chocolate for the bittersweet chocolate in the centers and for the coating, and use 1 cup whipping cream. Almonds go especially well with milk chocolate.

Praline Truffles
Substitute finely ground praline for the hazelnuts (see page 125).

Orange Chocolate Truffles

Yield: 60 1-inch round truffles

Orange and chocolate have a natural harmony. Candied orange peel imparts a chewy texture to these truffles.

Ingredients

1 pound bittersweet chocolate, finely chopped

1 1/2 cups whipping cream

4 tablespoons Grand Marnier or other orange-flavored liqueur

1 cup finely chopped candied orange peel,

plus 60 slivers candied orange peel (see page 184)

4 tablespoons cocoa powder

1 1/2 pounds bittersweet chocolate, to be tempered (see pages 24, 29-31)

Melt the chopped chocolate in the top of a double boiler over hot, not simmering, water, stirring frequently with a rubber spatula to ensure even melting. In a 1-quart saucepan over medium heat, bring the cream to a boil. Remove both pans from the heat, remove the top pan from the double boiler and wipe dry, pour the cream into the melted chocolate, and stir together until thoroughly blended. Stir in the Grand Marnier and the chopped candied orange peel. Transfer the mixture to a bowl, cover, let cool to room temperature, and chill in the refrigerator until thick but not stiff (2 to 3 hours).

Line 2 baking sheets with parchment or waxed paper. Fit a 12-inch pastry bag with a #5 large, plain round tip and fill partway with the truffle cream. Holding the pastry bag 1 inch above the paper, pipe out mounds about 1 inch in diameter. Cover the mounds with plastic wrap and chill in the freezer for 2 hours or 6 hours in the refrigerator.

Dust your hands with cocoa powder and roll the mounds into balls. These will be the truffle centers. Chill the centers for another 2 hours in the freezer.

Melt and temper the 1 1/2 pounds chocolate. Line 2 more baking sheets with parchment or waxed paper. Remove the truffle centers from the freezer 1 tray at a time. Place a truffle center into the tempered chocolate, coating it completely. With a dipper or fork remove the center from the chocolate, carefully shake off the excess chocolate, and turn the truffle out onto the paper. After dipping 4 centers, center a sliver of candied orange peel on top of each truffle before the chocolate sets up. Repeat with the remaining sheet of truffle centers.

Let the truffles set at room temperature or chill them in the refrigerator for 10 to 15 minutes. When the truffles are set place them in paper candy cups. In a tightly covered container wrapped in several layers of aluminum foil, the truffles will keep for 1 month in the refrigerator or 2 months in the freezer. The truffles are best served at room temperature.

Variations

Orange and Gold Truffles

Instead of placing slivers of candied orange peel on top of the truffles, use a small-tipped artist's brush to drop a few flakes of edible gold leaf on top of each truffle before the chocolate sets up. You will need 2 to 3 tablespoons of flecked edible gold leaf for each recipe.

White Chocolate Orange Truffles

Substitute white chocolate for the bittersweet chocolate in the centers and for the coating and use 3/4 cup whipping cream.

Milk Chocolate Orange Truffles

Substitute milk chocolate for the bittersweet chocolate in the centers and for the coating and use 1 cup whipping cream.

Tea Truffles

Yield: 60 1-inch round truffles

Tea adds a distinct yet mellow flavor to these uncommonly good truffles.

—————— Ingredients ——————

1 1/2 cups whipping cream

3 tablespoons loose oolong or green tea

1 pound bittersweet chocolate, finely chopped

3 to 4 tablespoons cocoa powder

1 1/2 pounds bittersweet chocolate, to be tempered (see pages 24, 29-31)

In a 1-quart saucepan over medium heat, bring the cream to a boil. Turn off the heat, add the loose tea, cover the pan, and allow to steep for 5 minutes. Strain the cream to remove the tea, then keep the cream warm in a covered saucepan.

Melt the chopped chocolate in the top of a double boiler over hot, not simmering, water, stirring frequently with a rubber spatula to ensure even melting. Remove the top pan from the double boiler and wipe it dry, pour the cream into the melted chocolate, and stir together until thoroughly blended. Transfer the mixture to a bowl, cover, let cool to room temperature, and chill in the refrigerator until thick but not stiff (2 to 3 hours).

Line 2 baking sheets with parchment or waxed paper. Fit a 12-inch pastry bag with a #5 large, plain round tip and fill partway with the truffle cream. Holding the pastry bag 1 inch above the paper, pipe out mounds about 1 inch in diameter. Cover the mounds with plastic wrap and chill in the freezer for 2 hours or in the refrigerator for 6 hours.

Dust your hands with cocoa powder and roll the mounds into balls. These will be the truffle centers. Cover and chill the centers for another 2 hours in the freezer.

Melt and temper the 1 1/2 pounds chocolate. Line 2 more baking sheets with parchment or waxed paper. Remove the truffle centers from the freezer 1 tray at a time. Place a truffle center into the tempered chocolate, coating it completely. With a dipper or fork remove the center from the chocolate, carefully shake off the excess chocolate, and turn the truffle out onto the paper. Repeat with the remaining sheet of truffle centers. After dipping the truffles place 2 tablespoons of the tempered chocolate in a paper pastry cone and snip off a tiny opening at the pointed end. Pipe the letter T on top of each truffle.

Let the truffles set at room temperature or chill them in the refrigerator for 10 to 15 minutes. When the truffles are set place them in paper candy cups. In a tightly covered container wrapped in several layers of aluminum foil, the truffles will keep for 1 month in the refrigerator or 2 months in the freezer. The truffles are best served at room temperature.

Variation

White Chocolate Tea Truffles

Substitute white chocolate for the bittersweet chocolate in the centers and for the coating, and use 3/4 cup whipping cream.

Mocha Truffles

Yield: 60 1-inch round truffles

Espresso coffee and chocolate are accented with coffee liqueur to produce a classic flavor combination. A candy coffee bean adorns the top of each truffle.

Ingredients

12 ounces bittersweet chocolate, finely chopped

4 ounces milk chocolate, finely chopped

1 1/4 cups whipping cream

1 1/2 tablespoons instant espresso powder

2 tablespoons Kahlua or other coffee-flavored liqueur

4 tablespoons cocoa powder

1 1/2 pounds bittersweet chocolate, to be tempered (see pages 24, 29-31)

60 candy coffee beans, for decoration

Melt the chopped bittersweet and milk chocolate in the top of a double boiler over hot, not simmering, water, stirring frequently with a rubber spatula to ensure even melting. In a 1-quart saucepan over medium heat, bring the cream to a boil. Remove the saucepan from the heat, dissolve the espresso powder in 3 tablespoons of the cream, then blend this mixture into the remaining cream. Remove the top pan from the double boiler, wipe it dry, pour the espresso cream into the melted chocolate, stir together until thoroughly blended, then stir in the Kahlua. Transfer the mixture to a bowl, cover, let cool to room temperature, and chill in the refrigerator until thick but not stiff (2 to 3 hours).

Line 2 baking sheets with parchment or waxed paper. Fit a 12-inch pastry bag with a #5 large, plain round tip and fill partway with the truffle cream. Holding the pastry bag 1 inch above the paper, pipe out mounds about 1 inch in diameter. Cover the mounds with plastic wrap and chill in the freezer for 2 hours or 6 hours in the refrigerator.

Dust your hands with cocoa powder and roll the mounds into balls. These will be the truffle centers. Chill the centers for another 2 hours in the freezer.

Melt and temper the 1 1/2 pounds chocolate. Line 2 baking sheets with parchment or waxed paper. Remove the truffle centers from the freezer 1 tray at a time. Place a truffle center into the tempered chocolate, coating it completely. With a dipper or fork remove the center from the chocolate, carefully shake off the excess chocolate, and turn the truffle out onto the paper. After dipping 4 centers, center a candy coffee bean on top of each truffle before the chocolate sets up. Repeat with the remaining sheet of truffle centers.

Let the truffles set at room temperature or chill them in the refrigerator for 10 to 15 minutes. When the truffles are set place them in paper candy cups. In a tightly covered container wrapped in several layers of aluminum foil, the truffles will keep for 1 month in the refrigerator or 2 months in the freezer. The truffles are best served at room temperature.

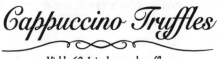

Cappuccino Truffles

Yield: 60 1-inch round truffles

Eating these truffles is like sipping a cup of rich cappuccino.

Ingredients

1 pound bittersweet chocolate, finely chopped

1 1/2 cups whipping cream

2 tablespoons instant espresso powder

1/2 teaspoon ground cinnamon

4 tablespoons confectioners' sugar

1 1/2 pounds white chocolate, to be tempered (see pages 24, 29-31)

60 candy coffee beans, for decoration

Melt the chopped chocolate in the top of a double boiler over hot, not simmering, water, stirring frequently with a rubber spatula to ensure even melting. In a 1-quart saucepan over medium heat, bring the cream to a boil. Remove the saucepan from the heat, dissolve the espresso powder in 3 tablespoons of the cream, then blend this mixture into the remaining cream. Stir in the ground cinnamon. Remove the top pan from the double boiler, wipe it dry, pour the cream into the melted chocolate, and stir together until thoroughly blended. Transfer the mixture to a bowl, cover, let cool to room temperature, and chill in the refrigerator until thick but not stiff (2 to 3 hours).

Line 2 baking sheets with parchment or waxed paper. Fit a 12-inch pastry bag with a #5 large, plain round tip and fill partway with the truffle cream. Holding the pastry bag 1 inch above the paper, pipe out mounds about 1 inch in diameter. Cover the mounds with plastic wrap and chill in the freezer for 2 hours or 6 hours in the refrigerator.

Dust your hands with confectioners' sugar and roll the mounds into balls. These will be the truffle centers. Chill the centers for another 2 hours in the freezer.

Melt and temper the white chocolate. Line 2 more baking sheets with parchment or waxed paper. Remove the truffle centers from the freezer 1 tray at a time. Place a truffle center into the tempered white chocolate, coating it completely. With a dipper or fork remove the center from the chocolate, carefully shake off the excess chocolate, and turn the truffle out onto the paper. After dipping 4 centers, center a candy coffee bean on top of each truffle before the chocolate sets up. Repeat with the remaining sheet of truffle centers.

Let the truffles set at room temperature or chill them in the refrigerator for 10 to 15 minutes. When the truffles are set place them in paper candy cups. In a tightly covered container wrapped in several layers of aluminum foil, the truffles will keep for 1 month in the refrigerator or 2 months in the freezer. The truffles are best served at room temperature.

Gianduja Truffles

Yield: 60 1-inch round truffles

Gianduja is a blend of chocolate and hazelnuts. By itself it is delicious. These truffles, with gianduja centers dipped in bittersweet chocolate, are like eating chocolate with a mild yet unmistakable flavor of hazelnuts.

Ingredients

12 ounces gianduja, finely chopped

4 ounces bittersweet chocolate, finely chopped

1 cup whipping cream

2 tablespoons Frangelico or other hazelnut-flavored liqueur

3/4 cup cocoa powder, divided

1 1/2 pounds bittersweet chocolate, to be tempered (see pages 24, 29-31)

Melt the gianduja and 4 ounces chopped chocolate together in the top of a double boiler over hot, not simmering, water, stirring frequently with a rubber spatula to ensure even melting. In a 1-quart saucepan over medium heat, bring the cream to a boil. Remove both pans from the heat, remove the top pan from the double boiler and wipe it dry, pour the hot cream into the melted chocolate, and stir together until thoroughly blended. Blend in the Frangelico. Transfer the mixture to a bowl, cover, let cool to room temperature, and chill in the refrigerator until thick but not stiff (2 to 3 hours).

Line 2 baking sheets with parchment or waxed paper. Fit a 12-inch pastry bag with a #5 large, plain round tip and fill partway with the truffle cream. Holding the pastry bag 1 inch above the paper, pipe out mounds about 1 inch in diameter. Cover the mounds with plastic wrap and chill in the freezer for 2 hours or 6 hours in the refrigerator.

Dust your hands with some of the cocoa powder and roll the mounds into balls. These will be the truffle centers. Chill the centers for another 2 hours in the freezer.

Melt and temper the 1 1/2 pounds chocolate. Line 2 more baking sheets with parchment or waxed paper. Remove the truffle centers from the freezer 1 tray at a time. Place a truffle center into the tempered chocolate, coating it completely. With a dipper or fork remove the center from the chocolate, carefully shake off the excess chocolate, and turn the truffle out onto the paper. After dipping 4 truffle centers, dust the tops of them lightly with the remaining cocoa powder before the chocolate sets up. Repeat with the remaining sheet of truffle centers.

Let the truffles set at room temperature or chill them in the refrigerator for 10 to 15 minutes. When the truffles are set place them in paper candy cups. In a tightly covered container wrapped in several layers of aluminum foil, the truffles will keep for 1 month in the refrigerator or 2 months in the freezer. The truffles are best served at room temperature.

Italian Gianduja Truffles

Yield: 60 1-inch round truffles

These truffles combine bittersweet chocolate with hazelnut and chocolate Nutella to create a smooth and distinct flavor.

Ingredients

1 pound bittersweet chocolate, finely chopped

2 cups Nutella (see page 10)

4 to 5 tablespoons cocoa powder

1 1/2 pounds bittersweet chocolate, to be tempered (see pages 24, 29-31)

3 ounces milk chocolate, to be tempered

Melt the chopped chocolate in the top of a double boiler over hot, not simmering, water, stirring frequently with a rubber spatula to ensure even melting. Remove the top pan from the double boiler, wipe it dry, and transfer the melted chocolate to a mixing bowl. Add the Nutella and stir together with a rubber spatula until thoroughly blended. Cover the bowl and chill in the refrigerator until thick but not stiff (30 minutes to 1 hour).

Line 2 baking sheets with parchment or waxed paper. Fit a 12-inch pastry bag with a #5 large, plain round tip and fill partway with the truffle cream. Holding the pastry bag 1 inch above the paper, pipe out mounds about 1 inch in diameter. Cover the mounds with plastic wrap and chill in the freezer for 20 minutes or 1 hour in the refrigerator.

Dust your hands with the cocoa powder and roll the mounds into balls. These will be the truffle centers. Chill the centers for another 20 minutes in the freezer.

Melt and temper the bittersweet and milk chocolate separately. Line 2 more baking sheets with parchment or waxed paper. Remove the truffle centers from the freezer 1 tray at a time. Place a truffle center into the tempered bittersweet chocolate, coating it completely. With a dipper or fork remove the center from the chocolate, carefully shake off the excess chocolate, and turn the truffle out onto the parchment paper. Place the tempered milk chocolate in a paper pastry cone and snip off a tiny opening at the end. Pipe several parallel lines across the tops of the truffles.

Let the truffles set at room temperature or chill in the refrigerator for 10 to 15 minutes. When the truffles are set place them in paper candy cups. In a tightly covered container wrapped in several layers of aluminum foil, the truffles will keep for 1 month in the refrigerator or 2 months in the freezer. The truffles are best served at room temperature.

Variation

Instead of dipping the truffles centers in the tempered chocolate, roll them in cocoa powder as soon as they are shaped into balls.

California Truffles

Yield: 60 1-inch round truffles

If you like almonds, these truffles are for you. California Truffles offer a bounty of almonds that are combined with dried apricots.

Ingredients

1 pound bittersweet chocolate, finely chopped

1 1/2 cups whipping cream

2 tablespoons Amaretto

2 teaspoons almond extract

1/2 cup finely chopped dried apricots, plus 60 slivers dried apricot

1/2 cup finely chopped almonds

4 tablespoons cocoa powder

1 1/2 pounds bittersweet chocolate, to be tempered (see pages 24, 29-31)

Melt the chopped chocolate in the top of a double boiler over hot, not simmering, water, stirring frequently with a rubber spatula to ensure even melting. In a 1-quart saucepan over medium heat, bring the cream to a boil. Remove both pans from the heat, remove the top pan from the double boiler and wipe it dry, pour the cream into the melted chocolate, and stir together until thoroughly blended. Stir in the Amaretto and almond extract, then blend in the chopped apricots and almonds. Transfer the mixture to a bowl, cover, let cool to room temperature, and chill in the refrigerator until thick but not stiff (2 to 3 hours).

Line 2 baking sheets with parchment or waxed paper. Fit a 12-inch pastry bag with a #6 large, plain round tip and fill partway with the truffle cream. Holding the pastry bag 1 inch above the paper, pipe out mounds about 1 inch in diameter. Cover the mounds with plastic wrap and chill in the freezer for 2 hours or 6 hours in the refrigerator.

Dust your hands with cocoa powder and roll the mounds into balls. These will be the truffle centers. Cover and chill the centers for another 2 hours in the freezer.

Melt and temper the 1 1/2 pounds chocolate. Line 2 more baking sheets with parchment or waxed paper. Remove the truffle centers from the freezer 1 sheet at a time. Place a truffle center into the tempered chocolate, coating it completely. With a dipper or fork remove the center from the chocolate, carefully shake off the excess chocolate, and turn the truffle out onto the paper. After dipping 4 centers, place a sliver of dried apricot on top of each truffle before the chocolate sets up. Repeat with the remaining sheet of truffle centers.

Let the truffles set at room temperature or chill them in the refrigerator for 10 to 15 minutes. When the truffles are set place them in paper candy cups. In a tightly covered container wrapped in several layers of aluminum foil, the truffles will keep for 1 month in the refrigerator or 2 months in the freezer. The truffles are best served at room temperature.

——————— Variation ———————

White Chocolate California Truffles
Substitute white chocolate for the bittersweet chocolate in the centers and for the coating, and use 3/4 cup whipping cream.

Gold Disks

Yield: 60 1-inch gold disks

These truffles are shaped into disks instead of balls, then dressed up with flakes of edible gold leaf for decoration. If the marvelous flavor doesn't impress your family and friends, the look of these truffles will.

Ingredients

1 pound bittersweet chocolate, finely chopped

1 1/2 cups whipping cream

3/4 cup toasted, skinned, and finely ground hazelnuts (see pages 32-33)

1 to 2 tablespoons cocoa powder

1 1/2 pounds bittersweet chocolate, to be tempered (see pages 24, 29-31)

4 tablespoons flaked edible gold leaf (see pages 9-10)

Melt the chopped chocolate in the top of a double boiler over hot, not simmering, water, stirring frequently with a rubber spatula to ensure even melting. In a 1-quart saucepan over medium heat, bring the cream to a boil. Remove both pans from the heat, remove the top pan from the double boiler and wipe it dry, pour the cream into the melted chocolate, and stir together until thoroughly blended. Mix in the hazelnuts and blend well. Transfer the mixture to a bowl, cover, let cool to room temperature, and chill in the refrigerator until thick but not stiff (2 to 3 hours).

Line 2 baking sheets with parchment or waxed paper. Fit a 12-inch pastry bag with a #5 large, plain round tip and fill partway with the truffle cream. Holding the pastry bag 1 inch above the paper, pipe out mounds about 1 inch in diameter. Dip your fingertips into cocoa powder and flatten the mounds into disks. Cover the truffle disks with plastic wrap and chill in the freezer for 2 hours or in the refrigerator for 6 hours. These will be the truffle centers.

Melt and temper the 1 1/2 pounds chocolate. Line 2 more baking sheets with parchment paper. Sprinkle the gold flakes over the paper. Remove the truffle centers from the freezer 1 sheet at a time. Place a truffle disk into the tempered chocolate, coating it completely. With a dipper or fork remove the center from the chocolate, carefully shake off the excess chocolate, and turn the disk out onto the gold flakes on the parchment paper. Let the truffle disks set at room temperature or chill them in the refrigerator for 10 to 15 minutes. Repeat with the remaining sheet of truffle disks. When the truffles disks are set, turn them over so that the gold flakes are on top, then place them in paper candy cups.

In a tightly covered container wrapped in several layers of aluminum foil, the gold disks will keep for 1 month in the refrigerator or 2 months in the freezer. The disks are best served at room temperature.

Variations

White Chocolate Gold Disks

Substitute white chocolate for the bittersweet chocolate in the centers and for the coating, and use 3/4 cup whipping cream.

Milk Chocolate Gold Disks

Substitute milk chocolate for the bittersweet chocolate in the centers and for the coating, and use 1 cup whipping cream for the centers. Almonds can be substituted for the hazelnuts.

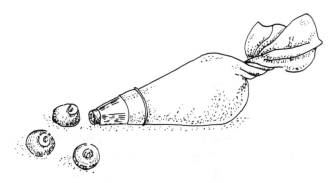

White Chocolate Apricot Truffles

Yield: 36 1-inch round truffles

White chocolate and apricot complement each other perfectly. The addition of apricot brandy or Cointreau gives these truffles a special zip.

Ingredients

4 tablespoons water, divided

2 tablespoons apricot brandy or Cointreau

1/2 cup dried apricots, finely chopped, plus 36 slivers dried apricot

6 tablespoons unsalted butter cut into small pieces

8 ounces white chocolate, finely chopped

1 large egg yolk, at room temperature

4 tablespoons confectioners' sugar

1 pound white chocolate, to be tempered (see pages 24, 29-31)

Place 2 tablespoons of the water and the 2 tablespoons brandy in a 1 quart saucepan and bring to a boil over medium-high heat. Stir in the chopped apricots, cover the pan, remove from the heat, and let stand until the liquid is absorbed (about 30 minutes).

Melt the butter in the top of a double boiler over hot, not simmering, water. Add the chopped white chocolate and the remaining 2 tablespoons water, and stir frequently with a rubber spatula while the chocolate melts. When the mixture is smooth, remove from the heat and blend in the egg yolk thoroughly. Transfer the mixture to the bowl of an electric mixer and beat until fluffy and cooled to room temperature (about 5 minutes). Stir in the chopped apricots, cover, and refrigerate until firm but not stiff (3 to 4 hours).

Line a baking sheet with parchment or waxed paper. With a spoon scoop out small mounds of the mixture. Dust your hands with confectioners' sugar and roll the mounds into 1 inch balls. These will be the truffle centers. Cover the truffle centers with plastic wrap and chill in the freezer for 2 hours or for 6 hours in the refrigerator.

Melt and temper the white chocolate. Line another baking sheet with parchment or waxed paper. Remove the sheet of truffle centers from the freezer, place a truffle center into the tempered chocolate, coating it completely. With a dipper or fork remove the center from the chocolate, carefully shake off the excess chocolate, and turn the truffle out onto the paper. After dipping 4 truffles, place a sliver of dried apricot on top of each truffle before the chocolate sets up.

Let the truffles set at room temperature or chill them in the refrigerator for 10 to 15 minutes. When the truffles are set place them in paper candy cups. In a tightly covered container wrapped in several layers of aluminum foil, the truffles will keep for 1 month in the refrigerator or 2 months in the freezer. The truffles are best served at room temperature.

--------------- Variations ---------------

Instead of dipping the truffle centers in white chocolate, roll them in finely chopped, toasted pistachio nuts as soon as they are formed into balls.

White Chocolate Pear Truffles

Substitute dried pears and Poire Williams pear brandy for the apricots and Cointreau.

Tropical Truffles

Yield: 60 1-inch round truffles

Lime zest, cream of coconut, and white chocolate are blended together to create a scrumptious flavor in these truffles. Cream of coconut is sold in cans, and is available in the baking or specialty foods section of most supermarkets, or in large liquor stores. Be sure to stir the cream of coconut thoroughly before using.

Ingredients

1/2 cup cream of coconut

2/3 cup whipping cream

1 tablespoon lime zest, finely diced

1 1/4 pounds white chocolate, finely chopped

1 tablespoon dark rum

1 teaspoon vanilla extract

4 tablespoons confectioners' sugar

1 1/2 pounds white chocolate, to be tempered (see pages 24, 29-31)

1/3 cup shredded coconut

Place the cream of coconut, cream, and lime zest in a 1-quart saucepan over medium heat, and bring to a boil. Remove from the heat, strain the mixture, and let cool for 10 minutes. At the same time, melt the chopped white chocolate in the top of a double boiler over hot, not simmering, water, stirring frequently with a rubber spatula to ensure even melting. Remove the top pan of the double boiler, wipe it dry, and add the cream mixture to the chocolate, blending thoroughly. Add the rum and vanilla extract, and stir to blend well. Transfer the mixture to a bowl, cover, let cool to room temperature, and refrigerate until thick but not stiff (4 to 6 hours).

Place the truffle cream in the bowl of an electric mixer and beat at medium speed until the mixture thickens and forms light peaks (about 1 minute). Do not beat too long or the mixture will curdle and become grainy.

Fit a 12-inch pastry bag with a #5 large, plain round tip and fill partway with the truffle cream. Line 2 baking sheets with parchment or waxed paper. Holding the pastry bag 1 inch above the paper, pipe out mounds 1 inch in diameter. Cover the mounds with plastic wrap and chill in the freezer for 2 hours or in the refrigerator for 6 hours.

Dust your hands with confectioners' sugar and roll the mounds into balls. These will be the truffle centers. Cover and chill the centers for another 2 hours in the freezer.

Melt and temper the 1 1/2 pounds white chocolate. Line 2 more baking sheets with parchment or waxed paper. Remove the truffle centers from the freezer 1 sheet at a time. Place a center into the tempered chocolate, coating it completely. With a dipper or fork remove the center from the chocolate, carefully shake off the excess chocolate, and turn the truffle out onto the paper. After dipping 4 truffles, sprinkle a pinch of shredded coconut on top of each truffle before the chocolate sets up. Repeat with the remaining sheet of truffle centers.

Let the truffles set at room temperature or chill them in the refrigerator for 10 to 15 minutes. When the truffles are set place them in paper candy cups. In a tightly covered container wrapped in several layers of aluminum foil, the truffles will keep for 1 month in the refrigerator or 2 months in the freezer. They are best served at room temperature.

Variation

Instead of dipping the truffle centers in tempered chocolate, roll them in confectioners' sugar or shredded coconut as soon as they are formed into balls.

Macadamia Nut Truffles

Yield: 60 1-inch truffles

The rich flavor of macadamia nuts balances very well with the delicate sweetness of white chocolate. A slightly crunchy texture adds to the delight of each bite of these truffles.

Ingredients

1 pound white chocolate, finely chopped

3/4 cup whipping cream

2 tablespoons Cognac

3/4 cup toasted, unsalted macadamia nuts, finely chopped, plus

1/4 cup toasted, unsalted macadamia nuts, finely ground

4 tablespoons confectioners' sugar

1 1/2 pounds white chocolate, to be tempered (see pages 24, 29-31)

Melt the chopped white chocolate in the top of a double boiler over hot, not simmering, water, stirring frequently with a rubber spatula to ensure even melting. In a 1-quart saucepan over medium heat, bring the cream to a boil. Remove both pans from the heat, remove the top pan of the double boiler, wipe it dry, and add the cream to the chocolate, blending thoroughly. Add the Cognac and chopped macadamia nuts, and stir to blend well. Transfer the mixture to a bowl, cover, let cool to room temperature, and refrigerate until thick but not stiff (3 to 4 hours).

Place the truffle cream in the bowl of a mixer and beat at medium speed until the mixture thickens and forms light peaks (about 1 minute). Do not beat too long or the mixture will curdle and become grainy.

Fit a 12-inch pastry bag with a #6 large, plain round tip and fill partway with the truffle cream. Line 2 baking sheets with parchment paper. Holding the pastry bag 1 inch above the paper, pipe out mounds 1 inch in diameter. Cover the mounds with plastic wrap and chill in the freezer for 2 hours or in the refrigerator for 6 hours.

Dust your hands with confectioners' sugar and roll the mounds into balls. These will be the truffle centers. Cover and chill the centers for another 2 hours in the freezer.

Melt and temper the 1 1/2 pounds white chocolate. Line 2 more baking sheets with parchment or waxed paper. Remove the truffle centers from the freezer 1 tray at a time. Place a center into the tempered chocolate, coating it completely. With a dipper or fork remove the center from the chocolate, carefully shake off the excess chocolate, and turn the truffle out onto the parchment paper. After dipping 4 truffles, sprinkle a pinch of the ground macadamia nuts on top of each truffle before the chocolate sets up. Repeat with the remaining sheet of truffle centers.

Let the truffles set at room temperature or chill them in the refrigerator for 10 to 15 minutes. When the truffles are set place them in paper candy cups. In a tightly covered container wrapped in several layers of aluminum foil, the truffles will keep for 1 month in the refrigerator or 2 months in the freezer. The truffles are best served at room temperature.

Variations

Instead of dipping the truffle centers in tempered chocolate, roll them in confectioners' sugar or finely ground macadamia nuts as soon as they are formed.

Pistachio Truffles

Substitute natural, toasted, unsalted pistachio nuts for the macadamia nuts.

Brazil Nut Truffles

Substitute toasted, unsalted Brazil nuts for the macadamia nuts.

White Chocolate Ginger Truffles

Yield: 60 1-inch truffles

The pungent flavor of crystallized ginger blends perfectly with the richness of white chocolate. These truffles have a slightly granular texture, which adds to the pleasure of eating them.

Ingredients

1 pound white chocolate, finely chopped

3/4 cup whipping cream

2 tablespoons Cognac

2 tablespoons finely chopped crystallized ginger, plus 60 slivers crystallized ginger

4 tablespoons confectioners' sugar

1 1/2 pounds white chocolate, to be tempered (see pages 24, 29-31)

Melt the chopped white chocolate in the top of a double boiler over hot, not simmering, water, stirring frequently with a rubber spatula to ensure even melting. In a 1-quart saucepan over medium heat, bring the cream to a boil. Remove both pans from the heat, remove the top pan of the double boiler, wipe it dry, and add the cream to the chocolate, blending thoroughly. Add the Cognac and the chopped crystallized ginger, and stir to blend well. Transfer the mixture to a bowl, cover, let cool to room temperature, and refrigerate until thick but not stiff (3 to 4 hours).

Place the truffle cream in the bowl of an electric mixer and beat at medium speed until the mixture thickens and forms light peaks (about 1 minute). Do not beat too long or the mixture will curdle and become grainy.

Fit a 12-inch pastry bag with a #6 large, plain round tip and fill partway with the truffle cream. Line 2 baking sheets with parchment or waxed paper. Holding the pastry bag 1 inch above the paper, pipe out mounds 1 inch in diameter. Cover the mounds with plastic wrap and chill in the freezer for 2 hours or in the refrigerator for 6 hours.

Dust your hands with confectioners' sugar and roll the mounds into balls. These will be the truffle centers. Cover and chill the centers for another 2 hours in the freezer.

Melt and temper the 1 1/2 pounds white chocolate. Line 2 more baking sheets with parchment or waxed paper. Remove the truffle centers from the freezer 1 tray at a time. Place a center into the tempered chocolate, coating it completely. With a dipper or fork remove the center from the chocolate, carefully shake off the excess chocolate, and turn the truffle out onto the paper. After dipping 4 truffles, place a sliver of crystallized ginger on top of each truffle before the chocolate sets up. Repeat with the remaining sheet of truffle centers.

Let the truffles set at room temperature or chill them in the refrigerator for 10 to 15 minutes. When the truffles are set place them in paper candy cups. In a tightly covered container wrapped in several layers of aluminum foil, the truffles will keep for 1 month in the refrigerator or 2 months in the freezer. The truffles are best served at room temperature.

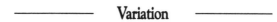

Variation

Instead of dipping the truffle centers in tempered chocolate, roll them in confectioners' sugar as soon as they are formed into balls.

Gianduja Truffle Cups

Truffle cream is piped into foil candy cups and chilled to form these delectable bite-sized candies. Before they are eaten, the foil cups are peeled away, leaving a fluted design in the chocolate.

Ingredients

8 ounces bittersweet chocolate, finely chopped

1 cup praline paste (see page 126)

60 whole hazelnuts, toasted and skinned (see pages 32-33)

Melt the chopped chocolate in the top of a double boiler over hot, not simmering, water, stirring frequently with a rubber spatula to ensure even melting. Remove the pan of chocolate from the water and wipe it dry. Add the praline paste to the chocolate and stir until smooth and thoroughly blended. Transfer the mixture to a bowl, cover, let cool to room temperature, and chill in the refrigerator until thick but not stiff (2 hours).

Fit a 12-inch pastry bag with a #5 large, plain round tip and fill partway with the truffle cream. Pipe the mixture into 1-inch foil candy cups until they are 3/4 full. Place a whole hazelnut, pointed end up, on top of the truffle cream and press it in lightly. Chill the truffle cups in the refrigerator until they are set (1 hour).

In a tightly covered container wrapped in several layers of aluminum foil, the truffle cups will keep for 1 month in the refrigerator or 2 months in the freezer. The truffle cups are best served at room temperature.

Mocha Ganache Truffle Cups

Yield: 60 1-inch truffle cups

These bite-sized candies blend espresso and chocolate to achieve a rich mocha flavor. They are terrific with after-dinner coffee.

Ingredients

8 ounces bittersweet chocolate, finely chopped

3/4 cup whipping cream

1 tablespoon instant espresso powder

60 candy mocha beans, for decoration

Melt the chopped chocolate in the top of a double boiler, over hot, not simmering, water, stirring frequently with a rubber spatula to ensure even melting.

In a 1-quart saucepan over medium heat, bring the cream to a boil. Remove from the heat, take 1 tablespoon of hot cream and dissolve the espresso powder in it, then blend into the remaining cream. Remove the top pan from the double boiler, wipe it dry, pour the hot cream into the melted chocolate, and stir the mixture until it is smooth and thoroughly blended. Transfer the mixture to a bowl, cover, let cool to room temperature, and chill in the refrigerator until thick but not stiff (2 to 3 hours).

Fit a 12-inch pastry bag with a #4 large, plain round tip. Fill the pastry bag partway with the ganache mixture. Pipe the mixture into 1-inch foil candy cups up to the top edge. Place a candy mocha bean on top of each cup. Chill the truffle cups until they are set (1 hour).

In a tightly covered container wrapped in several layers of aluminum foil, the truffle cups will keep for 1 month in the refrigerator or 2 months in the freezer. The truffle cups are best served at room temperature.

Hazelnut Ganache Cups

Yield: 60 1-inch ganache cups

Ingredients

8 ounces bittersweet chocolate, finely chopped

3/4 cup whipping cream

2/3 cup toasted, skinned, and finely ground hazelnuts,

plus 60 whole toasted and skinned hazelnuts (see pages 32-33)

Melt the chopped chocolate in the top of a double boiler, over hot, not simmering, water, stirring frequently with a rubber spatula to ensure even melting. In a 1-quart saucepan over medium heat, bring the cream to a boil. Remove both pans from the heat, remove the top pan from the double boiler and wipe it dry, and pour the cream into the melted chocolate. Stir the mixture until it is very smooth, then blend in the ground hazelnuts. Transfer the mixture to a bowl, cover, let cool to room temperature, and chill in the refrigerator until thick but not stiff (2 to 3 hours).

Fit a 12-inch pastry bag with a #5 large, plain round tip and fill partway with the ganache mixture. Pipe the mixture into 1-inch foil candy cups until they are 3/4 full. Place a whole hazelnut, pointed end up, on top of each ganache cup and press it in lightly. Chill the ganache cups until they are set (1 hour).

In a tightly covered container wrapped in several layers of aluminum foil, the ganache cups will keep for 1 month in the refrigerator or 2 months in the freezer. The ganache cups are best served at room temperature.

Variations

Any nuts can be substituted for the hazelnuts.

White Chocolate Hazelnut Ganache Cups

Substitute 10 ounces white chocolate for the bittersweet chocolate.

Milk Chocolate Hazelnut Ganache Cups

Substitute 9 ounces milk chocolate for the bittersweet chocolate.

More Chocolate Candies

*C*hocolate is a magical substance. It symbolizes richness and luxury. When added to other ingredients, countless delectable candies can be created. Almost everything goes with chocolate. Some of the more commonly used partners are nuts, candied fruits, coconut, and marzipan.

Chocolate has been around for centuries. The Mayas had cocoa plantations as early as 600 A.D. Columbus was the first European to discover the cocoa bean, and Cortez brought it back to the old world. The Europeans, especially the Italians and Swiss, elevated chocolate to great heights with their technological innovations and fanciful creations. Chocolate has been so highly valued that at times it has been used as currency. However, the real value comes from the sensational feeling one gets when eating chocolate. Rich and satisfying are two words that come to mind to describe the flavor that induces this feeling.

If you closely follow the directions given in each recipe, you too can easily create chocolate candies that are rich and satisfying. Before starting, be sure to set out all the equipment and measure out all the ingredients needed for each recipe. Handle chocolate with care to get the best results. Of course, use the best quality of chocolate as well as other ingredients called for. Because many recipes included in this chapter require tempered chocolate, make sure to read the section about tempering chocolate (see pages 24, 29-31) before beginning. Either regular chocolate or coverture (see page 7) can be used for dipping, coating, or molding any of the candies in this chapter.

A wide range of chocolate candies is offered in this chapter, including several types of clusters, handmade chocolate candy bars, *giandujas*, and molded filled chocolates. Most of the recipes offer variations. The variety of chocolate candies that can be made is virtually unlimited. A new candy can be created by merely changing the chocolate from one type to another. When you feel comfortable with these recipes, be creative and make your own masterpieces.

Chocolate candies store very well in the refrigerator. However, because chocolate is like a sponge, picking up other flavors easily, be careful where the candies are placed in the refrigerator. Also, moisture is the enemy of chocolate, so be sure to store the candies in an airtight container and, for extra protection, wrap the container in several layers of aluminum foil.

Chocolate candies can be frozen, but again, it is a good idea to cover the container with several layers of foil. If frozen, defrost the candies for 24 hours in the refrigerator before bringing them to room temperature to serve, since rapid temperature changes cause the chocolate to develop streaks or spots, and could possibly cause the outer coating to crack.

Chocolate candies taste best when eaten at room temperature. If they are too cold, their glorious full flavor cannot develop and be fully appreciated.

Orange Hazelnut Chocolate Clusters

Yield: 60 clusters

These scrumptious candies bring together three eminently compatible flavors: orange, hazelnut, and chocolate. For the best flavor be sure to use homemade candied orange peel. These clusters are easy to make and always receive rave reviews.

Ingredients

13 ounces bittersweet chocolate, finely chopped

2 cups finely chopped candied orange peel (see page 184), at room temperature

2 cups toasted, skinned, and finely chopped hazelnuts, chilled

Melt the chopped chocolate in the top of a double boiler over hot, not simmering, water, stirring frequently with a rubber spatula to ensure even melting. Remove the double boiler from the heat, remove the top pan containing the chocolate, wipe it dry, and set aside briefly. Replace the water in the bottom pan with lukewarm tap water, then set the pan of chocolate on top of this and stir gently to reduce the temperature of the chocolate (10 to 15 minutes). It will begin to get a bit thicker as it cools. If using a chocolate thermometer, it should register 95°F.

Again remove the top pan of chocolate from the water and replace the water in the bottom pan with tap water that is a few degrees warmer than the chocolate. Set the pan of chocolate over the pan with warm water. The warm water will hold the chocolate at the correct temperature so that it does not cool too fast.

Remove the chopped hazelnuts from the refrigerator and, in a bowl, mix them thoroughly with the chopped candied orange peel. Stir this mixture into the chocolate, making sure that the nuts and peel are thoroughly coated with the chocolate.

Line a baking sheet with parchment or waxed paper. Spoon out clusters 1 inch in diameter onto the sheet, leaving 1 inch of space between them. Let the clusters firm up at room temperature or chill them in the refrigerator for 15 minutes, then place them in paper candy cups. In a tightly covered container wrapped in several layers of aluminum foil, the clusters will keep for 1 month in the refrigerator or 2 months in the freezer. The clusters are best served at room temperature.

Chocolate Peanut Clusters

Yield: 60 clusters

Ingredients

12 ounces bittersweet chocolate, finely chopped

3 cups toasted, salted peanuts, roughly chopped, at room temperature

Melt the chopped chocolate in the top of a double boiler over hot, not simmering, water, stirring frequently with a rubber spatula to ensure even melting. Remove the double boiler from the heat, remove the top pan containing the chocolate, wipe it dry, and set aside briefly. Replace the water in the bottom pan with lukewarm tap water, set the pan of chocolate on top of this, and stir gently to reduce the temperature of the chocolate (10 to 15 minutes). It will begin to get a bit thicker as it cools. If using a chocolate thermometer, it should register 95°F.

Again remove the top pan of chocolate from the water and replace the water in the bottom pan with tap water that is a few degrees warmer than the chocolate. Set the pan of chocolate over the bottom pan with warm water. The warm water will hold the chocolate at the correct temperature so that it does not cool too fast. Stir the peanuts into the chocolate, making sure to thoroughly coat them with chocolate.

Line a baking sheet with parchment or waxed paper. Spoon out clusters 1 inch in diameter onto the sheet, leaving 1 inch of space between them. Let the clusters firm up at room temperature or chill them in the refrigerator for 15 minutes, then place them in paper candy cups. In a tightly covered container wrapped in several layers of aluminum foil, the clusters will keep for 1 month in the refrigerator or 2 months in the freezer. The clusters are best served at room temperature.

Variations

Substitute milk chocolate for the bittersweet chocolate. Substitute any lightly toasted nuts for the peanuts.

Chocolate Peanut Raisin Clusters

Substitute raisins for half of the peanuts.

Rochers

Yield: 60 pieces

Ingredients

12 ounces bittersweet chocolate, finely chopped

2 1/2 cups lightly toasted slivered almonds, at room temperature

1 cup lightly toasted shredded coconut, at room temperature

Melt the chopped chocolate in the top of a double boiler over hot, not simmering, water, stirring frequently with a rubber spatula to ensure even melting. Remove the double boiler from the heat, remove the top pan containing the chocolate, wipe it dry, and set aside briefly. Replace the water in the bottom pan with lukewarm tap water, set the pan of chocolate on top of this and stir gently to reduce the temperature of the chocolate (10 to 15 minutes). It will begin to get a bit thicker as it cools. If using a chocolate thermometer, it should register 95°F.

Again remove the top pan of chocolate from the water and replace the water in the bottom pan with tap water that is a few degrees warmer than the chocolate. Set the pan of chocolate over the bottom pan of warm water. The warm water will hold the chocolate at the correct temperature so that it does not cool too fast.

Mix the almonds and coconut together thoroughly, then blend them into the chocolate, making sure that they are thoroughly coated with chocolate.

Line a baking sheet with parchment or waxed paper. Spoon out clusters 1 inch in diameter onto the sheet, leaving 1 inch of space between them. Let the clusters firm up at room temperature or chill them in the refrigerator for 15 minutes, then place them in paper candy cups. In a tightly covered container wrapped in several layers of aluminum foil, the clusters will keep for 1 month in the refrigerator or 2 months in the freezer. The clusters are best served at room temperature.

Variation

Substitute milk chocolate for the bittersweet chocolate.

Tropical Clusters

Yield: 40 clusters

Macadamia nuts, dried pineapple, coconut, white chocolate, and a touch of crystallized ginger are blended to make these mouth-watering clusters. They are easy to prepare.

Ingredients

10 ounces white chocolate, finely chopped

2/3 cup sweetened condensed milk

1/2 cup toasted, unsalted macadamia nuts, roughly chopped

2 tablespoons finely chopped crystallized ginger

1/4 cup finely chopped dried pineapple

1/2 cup flaked or ribbon coconut

Melt the chopped chocolate in the top of a double boiler over hot, not simmering, water, stirring frequently with a rubber spatula to ensure even melting. In a 1-quart heavy-bottomed saucepan over medium heat, bring the sweetened condensed milk to a boil. Remove the double boiler from the heat, remove the top pan containing the chocolate, wipe it dry, and pour the hot milk into the chocolate. Blend together thoroughly.

In a 2-quart mixing bowl, blend the macadamia nuts, ginger, pineapple, and coconut together evenly. Pour in the chocolate and stir until the mixture is completely coated.

Line a baking sheet with parchment or waxed paper. Spoon out clusters 1 inch in diameter onto the sheet, leaving 1 inch of space between them. Place the baking sheet in the freezer until the clusters are firm (15 to 20 minutes). Place the clusters in paper candy cups.

In a tightly covered container wrapped in several layers of aluminum foil, the clusters will keep for 2 weeks in the refrigerator or 2 months in the freezer. The clusters are best served at room temperature.

Variations

Substitute 8 ounces bittersweet chocolate or 9 ounces milk chocolate for the white chocolate. Substitute any lightly toasted nuts for the macadamia nuts, and any dried fruit for the dried pineapple.

Hazelnut Chocolate Tuiles

Yield: 24 tuiles

Tuile is the French word for tile. The chocolate-nut mixture is draped over a rolling pin to give these confections a curve that resembles a roof tile. Tuiles can be presented in several ways. They are an attractive accompaniment to an assortment of other chocolates.

Ingredients

8 ounces bittersweet chocolate, finely chopped,

to be tempered (see pages 24, 29-31)

1 cup toasted, skinned, and finely ground hazelnuts

Cut 4 parchment paper sheets in half lengthwise; set aside. Prepare a stencil using a piece of cardboard 6 inches long by 4 inches wide. Draw a circle 2 1/2 inches in diameter in the upper half of the cardboard, then cut out the circle. The stencil is the cardboard with the circle removed.

Melt and temper the chocolate. Remove the top pan from the double boiler and wipe it dry, then stir in the ground hazelnuts thoroughly.

Set the stencil over a strip of parchment paper and spread about a tablespoon of the mixture over the opening, using an offset spatula with a 4-inch blade. The tuiles should be no more than 1/8 inch thick. Lift the stencil off the parchment paper and scrape the excess chocolate mixture from the stencil back into the bowl. You should be able to place 4 tuiles on each strip of parchment paper.

Let the tuiles set for 3 to 4 minutes, then carefully drape the parchment paper with the tuiles over a rolling pin that is set on a jelly roll pan. Chill the tuiles in the refrigerator until firm (10 to 15 minutes).

Gently peel the parchment paper off of the curved tuiles. In a tightly covered container wrapped in several layers of aluminum foil, the tuiles will keep for 1 week at room temperature or 1 month in the refrigerator. The tuiles are best served at room temperature.

Almond Chocolate Tuiles

Substitute 1 cup blanched, toasted, and finely ground almonds for the hazelnuts.

White Chocolate Tuiles

Substitute 10 ounces white chocolate for the bittersweet chocolate.

Coconut Chocolate Tuiles

Substitute 2 cups shredded coconut, lightly toasted, for the hazelnuts.

Chocolate Nut Bark

Yield: 10 to 14 pieces

For this confection you can use practically any combination of nuts or dried fruits, and any type of chocolate. Making bark is a good way to use up valuable leftover chocolate.

Ingredients

8 ounces chocolate (bittersweet, milk, or white),

to be tempered (see pages 24, 29-31)

1 cup whole nuts, toasted (almonds, hazelnuts, walnuts, macadamia nuts,

pecans, or pistachio nuts), at room temperature

Line a baking sheet with parchment or waxed paper. Melt and temper the 8 ounces chocolate. Stir the nuts into the chocolate, coating them completely. Turn the mixture out onto the baking sheet and spread it with an offset spatula to a thickness of 1/8 inch. Refrigerate to set the chocolate (15 to 20 minutes), then let the bark sit at room temperature for 30 minutes. Hold the bark with parchment or waxed paper and break it into pieces. This will prevent finger marks on the bark.

In a tightly covered container between layer of parchment or waxed paper, the bark will keep for 1 week at room temperature; if the container is wrapped in several layers of aluminum foil, the bark will keep for 1 month in the refrigerator. The bark is best served at room temperature.

Gianduja Diamonds

Yield: 126 diamonds

Ingredients

8 1/2 ounces milk chocolate, finely chopped

2 cups Nutella (see page 10) or

praline paste (see page 126), at room temperature, divided

9 1/2 ounces bittersweet chocolate, finely chopped

Line a baking sheet with parchment or waxed paper. Place a 4 1/2-inch by 14-inch flan ring in the center of the baking sheet.

Melt and temper the milk chocolate. Thoroughly mix in 1 cup of the Nutella, then pour this mixture into the flan ring. Use a rubber spatula to spread the mixture evenly into the corners and to an even thickness. Chill in the refrigerator for no more than 15 minutes.

Meanwhile, melt and temper the bittersweet chocolate. Thoroughly mix in the remaining cup of the Nutella and pour on top of the milk chocolate layer. Spread evenly with a rubber spatula. Chill the confection in the refrigerator until firm (2 to 3 hours). Remove the confection from the refrigerator. With a sharp, thin-bladed knife, cut around the rim of the flan ring to loosen it. Remove the flan ring, then gently peel the parchment paper off the back of the confection and place the confection on a cutting board. Cut into 1-inch-wide strips across the width. Lay each strip on its side and cut on the diagonal into pieces about 1/2-inch wide. Place 2 diamond-shaped pieces together in each paper candy cup.

In a tightly covered container wrapped in several layers of aluminum foil, the diamonds will keep for 1 month in the refrigerator or 2 months in the freezer. They are best served at room temperature.

Variation

Substitute 18 1/2 ounces gianduja chocolate for the milk chocolate and 1 cup of the Nutella or praline paste.

Gianduja Bars

Yield: 16 1-inch by 2-inch bars

You can't buy this candy bar in the store. Bittersweet chocolate, hazelnut paste, and chopped toasted hazelnuts are combined to create an incomparable flavor.

Ingredients

12 ounces bittersweet chocolate, to be tempered (see pages 24, 29-31), divided

1 3/4 cups praline paste (see page 126), at room temperature

3/4 cup toasted, skinned, and roughly chopped hazelnuts

Line a baking sheet with parchment or waxed paper. Place a 4 1/2-inch by 8 1/2-inch flan ring in the center of the paper.

Temper half the chocolate, then thoroughly blend in the praline paste. Stir in the hazelnuts. Pour this mixture into the flan ring and use a rubber spatula to spread it evenly and smoothly. Chill the confection in the refrigerator until firm (2 to 3 hours).

With a sharp, thin-bladed knife, cut around the rim of the flan ring to loosen and remove it. Leave the confection on the paper.

Temper the remaining 6 ounces chocolate and pour half of it on top of the confection. Spread it very rapidly with a flexible blade spatula, then use a pastry comb to make a textured design in the chocolate before it sets. Chill the confection in the refrigerator until the chocolate sets up (about 10 minutes).

Remove the confection from the refrigerator and invert it onto the paper. Use the remaining tempered chocolate to coat this side and use the pastry comb to make a design. Chill the confection in the refrigerator until the chocolate sets up (about 10 minutes).

Remove the confection from the refrigerator and let it sit at room temperature for 10 minutes. Cut the confection into 1-inch-wide bars across the width. Cut each bar in half across its width, which will make 1-inch by 2-inch bars. Place each bar in a paper candy cup.

In a tightly covered container wrapped in several layers of aluminum foil, the bars will keep for 1 month in the refrigerator or 2 months in the freezer. They are best served at room temperature.

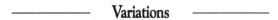

Variations

Substitute 14 ounces gianduja chocolate for 6 ounces of the bittersweet chocolate and the praline paste.

Almond Chocolate Bars

Substitute almond butter (see praline paste, page 126) and whole toasted almonds for the praline paste and the hazelnuts.

California Fruit & Nut Chocolate Bars

Yield: 28 1-inch by 2-inch bars

These candy bars are loaded with the best that California has to offer. Toasted almonds, candied orange peel, and raisins are combined to make a delicious chunky candy bar.

Ingredients

1 3/4 cups whole unblanched almonds, toasted

1/2 cup lightly toasted shredded coconut

3/4 cup roughly chopped candied orange peel (see page 184)

1/2 cup raisins

14 ounces bittersweet chocolate, to be tempered (see pages 24, 29-31)

Line a baking sheet with parchment or waxed paper. Place a 14-inch by 4 1/2-inch flan ring in the center of the paper.

In a 2-quart mixing bowl, combine the almonds, coconut, orange peel, and raisins; toss to blend evenly. Pour this mixture into the tempered chocolate and stir to coat it completely. Pour the chocolate mixture into the flan ring and use a rubber spatula to spread evenly and smoothly. Chill in the refrigerator until slightly set (about 15 minutes).

Remove from the refrigerator and score the candy into 1-inch-wide bars. Score each bar in half across its width, which will indicate 1-inch by 2-inch bars. Return the candy to the refrigerator to set completely (about 1 hour). Remove the candy from the refrigerator and let it stand at room temperature for 30 minutes.

With a sharp, thin-bladed knife, cut around the rim of the flan ring to remove it, then cut the candy into the marked pieces.

Place each bar in a paper candy cup. In a tightly covered container wrapped in several layers of aluminum foil, the bars will keep for 1 month in the refrigerator or 2 months in the freezer. They are best served at room temperature.

---- **Variations** ----

Substitute any nuts for the almonds. Substitute other dried fruits for the candied orange peel and raisins.

White Chocolate California Fruit and Nut Bars

Substitute white chocolate for the bittersweet chocolate.

California Fruit and Nut Chocolate Squares

Line an 8-inch square baking pan with aluminum foil that extends over the sides. Pour the chocolate fruit and nut mixture into the pan, chill, and mark into 1-inch squares instead of bars. *Yield: 64 1-inch squares*

Nougatine Triangles

Yield: 20 triangles

Ingredients

8 ounces bittersweet chocolate, finely chopped

3/4 cup whipping cream

1 recipe Nougatine (see page 136), cut into 20 1 1/2-inch circles and 40 1-inch squares

Melt the chopped chocolate in the top of a double boiler over hot, not simmering, water, stirring frequently with a rubber spatula to ensure even melting. In a 1-quart heavy-bottomed saucepan over medium heat, bring the cream to a boil. Remove both pans from the heat, remove the top pan from the double boiler and wipe it dry, pour the cream into the melted chocolate, and stir together until thoroughly blended. Transfer the mixture to a bowl, cover, let cool to room temperature, then chill in the refrigerator until thick but not stiff (2 to 3 hours).

Line a baking sheet with parchment or waxed paper. Place the nougatine circles on the baking sheet with 1 inch of space between them. Fit a 12-inch pastry bag with a #5 large, plain round tip and fill partway with the truffle cream. Holding the pastry bag 1 inch above the circle, pipe a 1-inch-high mound of truffle cream in the center of each circle. Lean 2 nougatine squares against the chocolate mound, making them touch at the top, to enclose the chocolate. Refrigerate the nougatine triangles until they are set (about 15 minutes). Place each triangle in a paper candy cup. In a tightly covered container wrapped in several layers of aluminum foil, the nougatine triangles will keep for 2 weeks in the refrigerator or 2 months in the freezer. Make sure to place a piece of parchment or waxed paper between each layer of the nougatine triangles. They will become soft and sticky if exposed to too much moist or humid air. The nougatine triangles are best served at room temperature.

Variation

Substitute Krokant (see pages 134-135) circles and squares for the Nougatine. Any truffle cream can be used for the chocolate mounds.

Nutella Surprises

Yield: 12 1-inch-deep candies

Chocolate encloses a surprise filling of creamy Nutella and a whole toasted hazelnut. You might want to make two batches of these popular confections.

Ingredients

12 ounces bittersweet chocolate, to be tempered (see pages 24, 29-31)

1/2 cup Nutella (see page 10)

12 toasted and skinned hazelnuts

Melt and temper the chocolate. In a 1-quart saucepan over low heat, heat the Nutella to lukewarm.

Remove the pan of Nutella from the heat. Pour the tempered chocolate into a paper pastry cone. Cut off a 1/2-inch opening at the end of the pastry cone. Pipe chocolate into each cavity of a 12-space, 1-inch-deep, spiral-topped chocolate mold. Tap the mold on a countertop a few times to eliminate air pockets. Turn the mold upside down over a sheet of parchment or waxed paper and let the chocolate run out. This will leave a thin film of chocolate coating each cavity of the mold. With a small flexible-blade spatula clean off the edges of each cavity of the mold.

Place a hazelnut in each cavity. Pour the Nutella into a paper pastry cone, cut off a 1/2-inch opening at the end, and pipe the Nutella into each cavity, filling it three quarters full. Pipe chocolate on top of the Nutella to fill each cavity just to the edge.

Place the mold in the freezer until the chocolate is set (15 minutes). Remove the mold from the freezer and turn it upside down over a piece of parchment or waxed paper. Hold the mold by opposite corners and gently twist it in opposite directions. The candies should drop out of the mold. If they don't drop out easily, return the mold to the freezer for another 15 minutes and try again. Place the candies in paper candy cups. In a tightly covered container wrapped in several layers of aluminum foil, the candies will keep for 2 weeks in the refrigerator or 2 months in the freezer. The candies taste best at room temperature.

Hazelnut Chocolate Kisses

Yield: 12 1-inch-deep candies

A whole toasted hazelnut surrounded by a rich filling of chocolate hazelnut truffle cream is the soul of these molded candies. They are similar to Italian Baci candies, only better.

Ingredients

6 ounces bittersweet chocolate, finely chopped

1/2 cup whipping cream

1/3 cup toasted, skinned, and finely ground hazelnuts

12 ounces bittersweet chocolate, to be tempered (see pages 24, 29-31)

12 toasted and skinned hazelnuts

Melt the chopped chocolate in the top of a double boiler over hot, not simmering, water, stirring frequently with a rubber spatula to ensure even melting. In a 1-quart heavy-bottomed saucepan over medium heat bring the cream to a boil. Remove both pans from the heat, remove the top pan from the double boiler and wipe it dry, pour the cream into the melted chocolate, and stir together until thoroughly blended. Mix in the ground hazelnuts and blend well. Transfer the mixture to a bowl, cover, let cool to room temperature, and chill in the refrigerator until thick but not stiff (2 to 3 hours).

Melt and temper the chocolate. Pour the tempered chocolate into a paper pastry cone and cut off a 1/2-inch opening at the pointed end of the cone. Pipe chocolate into each cavity of a 12-space, 1-inch-deep, spiral-topped chocolate mold. Tap the mold on a countertop a few times to eliminate air pockets. Turn the mold upside down over a sheet of parchment or waxed paper and let the chocolate run out. This will leave a thin film of chocolate coating each cavity of the mold. With a small flexible blade-spatula clean off the edges of each cavity of the mold.

Place a hazelnut in each cavity. Fit a 12-inch pastry bag with a #5 large, plain round tip and fill partway with the hazelnut truffle cream. Pipe the truffle cream into each cavity, filling it just below the top edge. Fill up the mold cavity with the remaining tempered chocolate. With a small flexible-blade spatula clean off the edges of each cavity, if necessary.

Place the mold in the freezer until the chocolate is set (15 minutes). Remove the mold from the freezer and turn upside down over a piece of parchment or waxed paper. Hold the mold by opposite corners and gently twist it in opposite directions. The candies should drop out of the mold. If they don't drop out easily, return the mold to the freezer for another 15 minutes and try again. Place the kisses in paper candy cups.

In a tightly covered container wrapped in several layers of aluminum foil, the kisses will keep for 1 month in the refrigerator or 2 months in the freezer. The kisses taste best at room temperature.

Variation

White Chocolate Hazelnut Kisses

Substitute white chocolate for the tempered bittersweet chocolate as the coating. For the truffle cream substitute 8 ounces white chocolate and 1/3 cup whipping cream for the 6 ounces bittersweet chocolate and 1/2 cup whipping cream.

Chocolate Almond Cups

Yield: 60 1-inch cups

If you like almonds, you will love these candies. Molded cups of chocolate surround a filling of rich almond truffle cream. Whole almonds adorn the top of these two-bite pieces of ecstasy.

Ingredients

8 ounces bittersweet chocolate, finely chopped

3/4 cup whipping cream

1/2 cup toasted and finely ground almonds, plus 60 whole blanched, toasted almonds

1 pound bittersweet chocolate, to be tempered (see pages 24, 29-31)

Melt the chopped chocolate in the top of a double boiler over hot, not simmering, water, stirring frequently with a rubber spatula to ensure even melting. In a 1-quart heavy-bottomed saucepan over medium heat, bring the cream to a boil. Remove both pans from the heat, remove the top pan from the double boiler and wipe it dry, pour the cream into the melted chocolate, and stir until thoroughly blended. Add the ground almonds and blend well. Transfer the mixture to a bowl, cover, let cool to room temperature, then chill in the refrigerator until thick but not stiff (2 to 3 hours).

Melt and temper the chocolate. Place the chocolate into a large paper pastry cone and cut off a 1/2-inch opening at the end. Pipe chocolate into 60 1-inch foil candy cups, filling them. Let the chocolate begin to set up around the edges for 5 minutes, then turn the cups upside down over a sheet of parchment or waxed paper and let the chocolate run out. This will leave a thin film of chocolate coating each cup.

Fit a 12-inch pastry bag with a #4 large, plain round tip and fill partway with the truffle cream. Pipe truffle cream into each foil cup to three quarters full. Pipe tempered chocolate into each cup, filling them to the top edge. Place a whole almond on top of each cup, pressing lightly so that it will adhere. Let the candies set at room temperature for 1 hour, or chill them in the refrigerator for 20 minutes.

In a tightly covered container wrapped in several layers of aluminum foil, the almond cups will keep for 1 month in the refrigerator or 2 months in the freezer. The candies taste best at room temperature.

Variations

Substitute any nuts for the almonds. Praline (see page 125) can be substituted for the nuts.

White Chocolate Nut Cups

For the filling substitute 10 ounces white chocolate and 1/2 cup whipping cream for the 8 ounces bittersweet chocolate and 3/4 cup whipping cream. Use white chocolate to coat and top the cups.

Double Chocolate Nut Cups

Use white chocolate nut truffle cream for the filling.

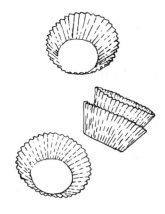

Extraordinary Candy Bars

Yield: 2 7-inch by 3-inch bars, or 4 3 1/2-inch by 2-inch bars

There are many molds available in bar shapes. Some are large rectangles with small segments that break apart; some are partially rounded rectangles; others are one piece. Whatever mold you choose, numerous different chocolate fillings can be used to create exciting and unusual candy bars.

Ingredients

6 ounces bittersweet chocolate, to be tempered (see pages 24, 29-31)

3 tablespoons finely ground Krokant (see page 134)

Melt and temper the chocolate, then stir the Krokant into the chocolate and blend thoroughly. Pour the mixture into the cavities of the mold of your choice, then clean off the edges with a flexible-blade spatula. Tap the mold on a countertop a few times to eliminate air pockets.

Place the mold on a flat surface in the freezer for 15 minutes. Remove the mold from the freezer and turn upside down over a piece of parchment or waxed paper. Hold the mold by opposite corners and gently twist it in opposite directions. The candy bars should drop out of the mold. If they don't drop out easily, return the mold to the freezer for another 15 minutes and try again.

In a tightly covered container, the molded chocolate bars will keep for 1 week at room temperature; if the container is wrapped in several layers of aluminum foil, the bars will keep for 1 month in the refrigerator or 2 months in the freezer. The chocolate bars taste best at room temperature.

Variations

Substitute Nougatine (see page 136) for the Krokant. Praline (see page 125) can replace the Nougatine or Krokant.

White Chocolate Pecan Bars

Substitute 10 ounces tempered white chocolate for 12 ounces tempered bitter-sweet chocolate, and 2/3 cup toasted and roughly chopped pecans for the Krokant. *Yield: 64 1/2-inch by 1 1/2 inch bars*

Chocolate Hazelnut Bars

Substitute 6 ounces milk or white chocolate for the bittersweet chocolate and 3 tablespoons finely ground toasted hazelnuts for the Krokant.

Chocolate Almond Bars

Substitute 6 ounces milk or white chocolate for the bittersweet chocolate and 1/2 cup whole unblanched, toasted almonds for the Krokant.

Any nuts can be substituted. Praline (see page 125) can be substituted for the nuts.

Chocolate Hearts

Yield: 18 1-inch hearts

These molded, solid-chocolate hearts wrapped in red foil, or covered with edible gold leaf, are an impressive declaration of love.

Ingredients

8 ounces bittersweet chocolate, to be tempered (see pages 24, 29-31)

Temper the chocolate, then pour it into a large paper pastry cone. Cut off a 1/4-inch-wide opening at the end of the cone, and pipe chocolate into the cavities of a mold with 18 1-inch-wide hearts. With a flexible-blade spatula, clean around the edges of each cavity, if necessary. Tap the mold on a countertop a few times to eliminate air pockets. Place the mold on a flat surface in the freezer for 15 minutes, then remove the mold from the freezer and turn upside down over a piece of parchment or waxed paper. Hold the mold by opposite corners and gently twist it in opposite directions. The chocolate hearts should drop out of the mold. If they don't drop out easily, return the mold to the freezer for another 15 minutes and try again.

Wrap each chocolate heart in a square of red foil or delicately place a half sheet of edible gold leaf onto each heart. Use a thin sable brush to fit the gold leaf around the heart. Avoid touching the gold leaf; it will stick to your hands.

In a tightly covered container, the chocolate hearts will keep for 1 week at room temperature; if the container is wrapped in several layers of aluminum foil, the hearts will keep for 1 month in the refrigerator or 2 months in the freezer. The edible gold leaf will dissolve if exposed to too much moist or humid air. The chocolate hearts taste best at room temperature.

Variations

3 tablespoons of any lightly toasted, finely ground nuts can be blended into the chocolate before molding.

Substitute white chocolate or milk chocolate for the bittersweet chocolate.

Any shapes can be used for solid molding.

Caramel
Candies

*C*aramels are rich, creamy, and very chewy candies. They are made primarily with sugar, corn syrup, honey, milk, cream, and butter. Nuts and other ingredients are added for texture and to enhance the flavor of the caramels. Their distinctive flavor and color is the result of the caramelization of sugar and milk products.

Because caramels must be cooked for 10 to 15 minutes, it is best to use a heavy-bottomed saucepan to help prevent scorching and a long-handled wooden spoon for stirring often to prevent burning. It's important to pay attention when cooking caramels, because as the batch reaches its finishing point, it becomes thick and must be stirred constantly.

When the caramel mixture is removed from the heat, it is necessary to quickly blend in the remaining ingredients before turning the mixture into the prepared pan. Stirring the mixture too much at this time will make the caramels grainy. Also, don't scrape out the pan. What remains in the pan after pouring has a slightly different texture from that of the caramel mixture, because it was closer to the heat and cooked more. Adding this to the caramel mixture would leave hard spots in the candies.

After the caramels are cooked, they must be allowed to cool completely at room temperature before they are cut. This takes anywhere from 2 hours to overnight, depending on the recipe. Caramels are sticky and difficult to cut if they are cut too soon. The best way to cut caramels is with a large chef's knife. The blade of the knife should be oiled with a tasteless vegetable oil, such as safflower oil. A sawing motion should be used to cut through the caramels. If the cutting becomes too difficult, oil the blade of the knife again.

For storing, caramels can be individually wrapped in waxed paper or plastic wrap, with the ends twisted. They also can be stored unwrapped between pieces of waxed paper in a tightly covered container. Be sure to leave space between them if they are stored in this manner, so they don't stick together. Because caramels absorb moisture easily, they should not be stored in the refrigerator.

There are several delectable recipes for caramel candies in this chapter. If you really want to dress up caramels, you can dip them in tempered bittersweet or milk chocolate. Whether you choose to make plain caramels, nut caramels, or caramels dipped in chocolate, you are guaranteed to have a hit.

Vanilla Cream Caramels

Yield: 64 pieces

These are chewy caramels with the rich, mellow flavor of pure vanilla.

Ingredients

2 tablespoons tasteless vegetable oil, such as safflower oil, divided

1 1/2 cups whipping cream

1 1/2 cups sugar

1/3 cup honey

1 vanilla bean, split lengthwise

3 tablespoons unsalted butter, softened

Line an 8-inch square baking pan with aluminum foil that extends over the sides. With a paper towel coat the bottom and sides of the foil with 1 tablespoon of the vegetable oil; set aside.

In a 3-quart heavy-bottomed saucepan over medium heat, combine the cream, sugar, honey, and vanilla bean, and stir until the sugar is dissolved (about 5 minutes). Wash down the sides of the pan 2 times with a pastry brush dipped in warm water, to prevent the sugar from crystallizing.

Increase the heat to medium-high and bring the mixture to a boil. Place a candy thermometer in the pan and cook the mixture until it registers 250°F on the thermometer (10 to 15 minutes), stirring frequently.

Remove the pan from the heat; with a fork remove the vanilla bean from the mixture, stir in the butter, and pour the mixture into the prepared pan. Let the caramel cool completely at room temperature (2 to 3 hours).

With the remaining tablespoon of vegetable oil, coat a cutting board and the blade of a large chef's knife. Remove the candy from the pan by lifting out the foil; invert the caramel onto the cutting board and peel the foil off the caramel. Cut the caramel into 8 1-inch-wide strips and cut each strip into 8 1-inch squares. In a tightly covered container, between sheets of waxed paper, or wrapped in waxed paper squares, the caramels will keep for 2 weeks at room temperature.

Classic Cream Caramels

Yield: 112 pieces

These are truly the quintessential caramel. They are chewy and creamy and just plain good.

─────── **Ingredients** ───────

2 tablespoons tasteless vegetable oil, such as safflower oil, divided

2 cups sugar

1 cup light corn syrup

2 tablespoons unsalted butter, softened, cut into pieces, divided

2 cups whipping cream

1/2 teaspoon salt

2 teaspoons vanilla extract

Line a baking sheet with aluminum foil, then place a 14-inch by 4 1/2-inch flan ring in the center of the foil. With a paper towel coat the foil and the inside of the flan ring with 1 tablespoon of the vegetable oil; set aside.

In a 4-quart heavy-bottomed saucepan over medium heat, combine the sugar and corn syrup, and stir constantly until the mixture comes to a boil (about 5 minutes). Wash down the sides of the pan 2 times with a pastry brush dipped in warm water, to prevent the sugar from crystallizing.

Place a candy thermometer in the pan, increase the heat to medium-high, and cook the mixture, without stirring, until it registers 305°F on the thermometer (about 15 minutes).

Remove the pan from the heat and stir in 1 tablespoon of the butter. Return the pan to the heat and add the remaining tablespoon of butter, a little at a time, keeping the mixture boiling.

In a 1-quart saucepan over medium heat, heat the cream. Slowly add the cream to the caramel mixture and continue cooking until the mixture registers 250°F on the thermometer (about 10 minutes), stirring vigorously.

*This temperature will result in candy which requires a hammer and chisel to serve. Softer caramels to 235°F, firmer to 240-245°F

◆ Butter Nut Caramels (top left) (page 112), Chocolate Hazelnut Nougat (page 170) ◆
and White Chocolate Almond Bark (bottom right) (page 86)

◆ *Peanut Brittle* ◆
(page 127)

◆ *Turtles (page 121)* ◆

◆ *White Chocolate Apricot Truffles* (page 66) ◆

◆ *Hazelnut Chocolate Tuiles (page 84)* ◆

◆ *Hazelnut Chocolate Truffles (page 48)* ◆

◆ *English Toffee (page 130)* ◆

◆ *Chocolate Nut Bark (page 86)* ◆

◆ *Classic Chocolate Truffles (page 42)* ◆

◆ (top row, left to right) Gianduja (pg. 58), Chocolate-Dipped Apricots (pg. 180), ◆
Nougatine (pp. 136-137), Nougatine Triangles (pg. 92),Chocolate-Dipped
Candied Orange Peel (pp. 184-185) and Candied Orange Peel (pp. 184-185),
Chocolate Caramels (pg. 111)

(center, left to right) Chocolate Orange Marzipan Hearts (pp. 149-150) and Orange
Marzipan Hearts (pp. 149-150)

(bottom row, left to right) Krokant and Chocolate-Dipped Krokant (pp.134-135),
Hazelnut Ganache Cups (pg. 76), Classic Cream Caramels (pp. 104-105),
(bottom) Orange Hazelnut Chocolate Clusters (pg.79), (top) Raspberry Chocolate
Truffles (pp. 46-47)

◆ *Gold Disks (page 64-65)* ◆

Remove the pan from the heat and let it stand for 5 minutes, then stir in the salt and vanilla. Pour the caramel into the prepared flan ring and let it sit for 8 hours at room temperature.

With the remaining tablespoon of vegetable oil, coat a cutting board and the blade of a large chef's knife. With the knife, loosen and remove the flan ring, invert the caramel onto the cutting board, and peel the foil off the caramel. Cut the caramel into 1/2-inch-wide strips across the width, then cut each strip into 4 pieces. In a tightly covered container, between sheets of waxed paper, or wrapped in waxed paper rectangles, the caramels will keep for 2 weeks at room temperature.

Variation

Classic Nut Cream Caramels

Add 1 cup roughly chopped nuts to the caramel mixture when adding the salt and vanilla.

Brown Sugar Caramels

Yield: 64 pieces

The brown sugar used to make these caramels greatly heightens their flavor.

Ingredients

2 tablespoons tasteless vegetable oil, such as safflower oil, divided

3/4 cup firmly packed light brown sugar

1/4 cup granulated sugar

3/4 cup light corn syrup

3/4 cup sweetened condensed milk

4 tablespoons unsalted butter, softened

Pinch of salt

Line an 8-inch square baking pan with aluminum foil that extends over the sides. With a paper towel coat the bottom and sides of the foil with 1 tablespoon of the vegetable oil; set aside.

In a 3-quart heavy-bottomed saucepan over medium heat, combine the brown sugar, granulated sugar, corn syrup, milk, butter, and salt. Stir with a wooden spoon until the mixture comes to a boil (5 to 8 minutes). Wash down the sides of the pan 2 times with a pastry brush dipped in warm water, to prevent the sugar from crystallizing.

Increase the heat to medium-high, place a candy thermometer in the pan, and cook the mixture until it registers 240°F on the thermometer (10 to 15 minutes), stirring constantly.

Remove the pan from the heat and pour the mixture into the prepared pan. Let the caramel cool completely at room temperature (8 hours or overnight).

With the remaining tablespoon of vegetable oil, coat a cutting board and the blade of a large chef's knife. Remove the candy from the pan by lifting out the foil; invert the caramel onto the cutting board and peel the foil off the caramel. Cut the caramel into 8 1-inch-wide strips, then cut each strip into 8 pieces. In a tightly covered container, between sheets of waxed paper, or wrapped in waxed paper squares, the caramels will keep for 2 weeks at room temperature.

Variation

Add 1 cup roughly chopped toasted nuts to the caramel mixture before pouring into the prepared pan.

Peanut Caramels

Yield: *112 pieces*

These candies resemble the candy bars I used to buy at the movies when I was a child. They are nutty, crunchy, and coated with chocolate.

Ingredients

2 tablespoons tasteless vegetable oil, such as safflower oil, divided

1/2 cup granulated sugar

1/2 cup firmly packed light brown sugar

3/4 cup light corn syrup

1 cup whipping cream

1 tablespoon unsalted butter, softened

2 teaspoons vanilla extract

1 1/2 cups toasted, salted peanuts

1 pound bittersweet chocolate, to be tempered (see pages 24, 29-31)

Line a baking sheet with aluminum foil, then place a 14-inch by 4 1/2-inch flan ring in the center of the foil. With a paper towel coat the foil and the inside of the flan ring with 1 tablespoon of the vegetable oil; set aside.

In a 3-quart heavy-bottomed saucepan over medium heat, combine the granulated sugar, brown sugar, corn syrup, cream, and butter. Stir with a wooden spoon until the mixture comes to a boil (5 to 8 minutes). Wash down the sides of the pan 2 times with a pastry brush dipped in warm water, to prevent the sugar from crystallizing.

Increase the heat to medium-high, place a candy thermometer in the pan, and cook the mixture until it registers 246°F on the thermometer (15 to 20 minutes), stirring constantly.

Remove the pan from the heat; stir in the vanilla, then blend in the peanuts. Pour the mixture into the prepared flan ring and spread it out rapidly with a wooden spoon. Let the caramel cool completely at room temperature (2 to 3 hours).

With the remaining tablespoon of vegetable oil, coat a cutting board and the blade of a large chef's knife. With the knife, loosen and remove the flan ring; invert the caramel onto the cutting board, and peel the foil off the caramel. Cut the caramel into 1/2-inch-wide strips across the width, then cut each strip into 4 pieces.

Melt and temper the chocolate. Line 2 baking sheets with parchment or waxed paper. Dip a piece of the peanut caramel into the chocolate, coating it completely. With a fork or dipper, remove the caramel from the chocolate, shaking off the excess chocolate, and turn the piece out onto the paper. Repeat with the remaining pieces. Let the chocolate set at room temperature or chill in the refrigerator for 15 minutes. When the candies are set, place them in paper candy cups. In a tightly covered container wrapped in several layers of aluminum foil, the caramels will keep for 1 month in the refrigerator or 2 months in the freezer. They are best eaten at room temperature.

 Variations

Substitute any nuts for the peanuts.
Substitute milk chocolate for the bittersweet chocolate.

Honey Nut Caramels

Yield: 64 pieces

Ingredients

2 tablespoons tasteless vegetable oil, such as safflower oil, divided

1 cup whipping cream

1 1/4 cups sugar

3 tablespoons honey

1/2 vanilla bean, split lengthwise

1 tablespoon unsalted butter, softened

1/2 cup roughly chopped toasted cashews or other toasted nuts

Line a baking sheet with aluminum foil, then place an 8-inch by 4 1/2-inch flan ring in the center of the foil. With a paper towel coat the foil and the inside of the flan ring with 1 tablespoon of the vegetable oil; set aside.

In a 2-quart heavy-bottomed saucepan over medium heat, bring the cream to a boil. Add the sugar, honey, and vanilla bean, and return the mixture to a boil. Wash down the sides of the pan 2 times with a pastry brush dipped in warm water, to prevent the sugar from crystallizing.

Increase the heat to medium-high, place a candy thermometer in the pan, and cook the mixture until it registers 253°F on the thermometer (10 to 15 minutes), stirring occasionally. Remove the pan from the heat; with a fork remove the vanilla bean from the mixture, stir in the butter, then blend in the cashews. Pour the mixture into the prepared flan ring. Let the caramel cool completely at room temperature (2 to 3 hours).

With the remaining tablespoon of vegetable oil, coat a cutting board and the blade of a large chef's knife. With the knife, loosen and remove the flan ring, invert the caramel onto the cutting board, and peel the foil off the caramel. Cut the caramel into 1/2-inch-wide strips across the width, then cut each strip into 4 pieces. In a tightly covered container, between sheets of waxed paper, or wrapped in waxed paper squares, the caramels will keep for 2 weeks at room temperature.

Chocolate Caramels

Yield: 64 pieces

Bittersweet chocolate gives these caramels their terrific flavor.

Ingredients

2 tablespoons tasteless vegetable oil, such as safflower oil, divided

1 1/2 cups whipping cream

10 ounces bittersweet chocolate, finely chopped

2 cups sugar

1/2 cup honey

2 tablespoons unsalted butter, softened

Line an 8-inch square baking pan with aluminum foil that extends over the sides. With a paper towel coat the bottom and sides of the foil with 1 tablespoon of the vegetable oil; set aside.

In a 3-quart heavy-bottomed saucepan over medium heat, bring the cream to a boil. Add the chocolate and stir until it is melted and thoroughly blended (about 3 minutes). Add the sugar and honey. Return the mixture to a boil, and wash down the sides of the pan 2 times with a pastry brush dipped in warm water, to prevent the sugar from crystallizing.

Place a candy thermometer in the pan and cook the mixture until it registers 257°F on the thermometer (8 to 10 minutes), stirring constantly.

Remove the pan from the heat; stir in the butter, then pour the mixture into the prepared pan. Let the caramel cool completely at room temperature (2 to 3 hours).

With the remaining tablespoon of vegetable oil, coat a cutting board and the blade of a large chef's knife. Remove the candy from the pan by lifting out the foil; invert the caramel onto the cutting board, and peel the foil off the caramel. Cut the caramel into 8 1-inch-wide strips, then cut each strip into 8 pieces. In a tightly covered container, between sheets of waxed paper, or wrapped in waxed paper squares, the caramels will keep for 2 weeks at room temperature.

Butter Nut Caramels

Yield: 112 pieces

These caramels are my favorites. They are creamy, chewy, and loaded with nuts.

Ingredients

2 tablespoons tasteless vegetable oil, such as safflower oil, divided

3/4 cup whole milk

1/2 cup whipping cream

3/4 cup sweetened condensed milk

1 cup light corn syrup

2 cups sugar

1/2 cup unsalted butter, softened, cut into pieces

1 teaspoon vanilla extract

1 cup roughly chopped toasted whole almonds

Line a baking sheet with aluminum foil, then place a 14-inch by 4 1/2-inch flan ring in the center of the foil. With a paper towel coat the foil and the inside of the flan ring with 1 tablespoon of the vegetable oil.

In a 3-quart heavy-bottomed saucepan over medium heat, combine the whole milk, cream, condensed milk, corn syrup, sugar, and butter. Stir until the mixture comes to a boil (5 to 8 minutes). Wash down the sides of the pan 2 times with a pastry brush dipped in warm water, to prevent the sugar from crystallizing.

Increase the heat to medium-high, place a candy thermometer in the pan, and cook the mixture until it registers 240°F on the thermometer (15 to 20 minutes), stirring constantly.

Remove the pan from the heat; stir in the vanilla, then blend in the chopped almonds. Pour the mixture into the prepared flan ring and spread it out rapidly with a wooden spoon. Let the caramel cool completely at room temperature (2 to 3 hours).

With the remaining tablespoon of vegetable oil, coat a cutting board and the blade of a large chef's knife. With the knife loosen and remove the flan ring, invert the caramel onto the cutting board, and peel the foil off the caramel. Cut the caramel into 1/2-inch-wide strips across the width, then cut each strip into 4 pieces. In a tightly covered container, between sheets of waxed paper, or wrapped in waxed paper squares, the caramels will keep for 2 weeks at room temperature.

Variation

Substitute any nuts for the almonds.

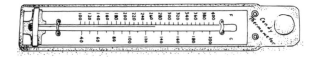

Orange Caramels

Yield: 64 pieces

Orange zest—the orange skin, not the white pith—gives a fresh, exciting flavor to these chewy candies.

Ingredients

2 tablespoons tasteless vegetable oil, such as safflower oil, divided

Zest of 2 large oranges, finely diced

1/2 cup water

2 1/4 cups sugar, divided

1 1/2 cups whipping cream

1/3 cup honey

2 tablespoons unsalted butter, softened

Line an 8-inch square baking pan with aluminum foil that extends over the sides. With a paper towel coat the bottom and sides of the foil with 1 tablespoon of the vegetable oil; set aside.

In a 1-quart heavy-bottomed saucepan over medium-high heat, combine the orange zest, the water, and 3/4 cup of the sugar, and bring to a boil. Remove the pan from the heat, cover, and let stand for 10 minutes.

In a 3-quart heavy-bottomed saucepan over medium heat, bring the cream to a boil. Add the remaining 1 1/2 cups sugar and the honey, and return the mixture to a boil. Wash down the sides of the pan 2 times with a pastry brush dipped in warm water, to prevent the sugar from crystallizing.

Place a candy thermometer in the pan, increase the heat to medium-high, and cook the mixture until it registers 240°F on the thermometer (8 to 10 minutes), stirring frequently. Add the orange sugar syrup and continue cooking the mixture until it registers 257°F on the thermometer.

Remove the pan from the heat; stir in the butter, then pour the mixture into the prepared pan. Let the caramel cool completely at room temperature (2 to 3 hours).

With the remaining tablespoon of vegetable oil, coat a cutting board and the blade of a large chef's knife. Remove the candy from the pan by lifting out the foil; invert the caramel onto the cutting board and peel the foil off the caramel. Cut the caramel into 8 1-inch-wide strips, then cut each strip into 8 pieces. In a tightly covered container, between sheets of waxed paper, or wrapped in waxed paper squares, the caramels will keep for 2 weeks at room temperature.

Maple Pecan Caramels

Yield: 64 pieces

These caramels combine maple syrup and pecans to produce a potent flavor that is hard to surpass. Be sure to use pure maple syrup.

Ingredients

2 tablespoons tasteless vegetable oil, such as safflower oil, divided

1 1/2 cups pure maple syrup

2 cups firmly packed light brown sugar

1/2 cup whipping cream

1 tablespoon unsalted butter, softened

1 cup roughly chopped toasted pecans

Line an 8-inch square baking pan with aluminum foil that extends over the sides. With a paper towel coat the bottom and sides of the foil with 1 tablespoon of the vegetable oil; set aside.

In a 3-quart heavy-bottomed saucepan over medium-high heat, combine the maple syrup, brown sugar, and cream, and bring to a boil, stirring frequently. Wash down the sides of the pan 2 times with a pastry brush dipped in warm water, to prevent the sugar from crystallizing.

Place a candy thermometer in the pan and cook the mixture until it registers 242°F on the thermometer (10 to 15 minutes), stirring constantly.

Remove the pan from the heat; stir in the butter, then blend in the pecans. Pour the mixture into the prepared pan. Let the caramel cool completely at room temperature (2 to 3 hours).

With the remaining tablespoon of vegetable oil, coat a cutting board and the blade of a large chef's knife. Remove the candy from the pan by lifting out the foil; invert the caramel onto the cutting board, and peel the foil off the caramel. Cut the caramel into 8 1-inch-wide strips, then cut each strip into 8 pieces. In a tightly covered container, between sheets of waxed paper, or wrapped in waxed paper squares, the caramels will keep for 2 weeks at room temperature.

Variations

Substitute walnuts, Brazil nuts, or almonds for the pecans.

Espresso Caramels

Espresso adds extra zip to the rich flavor of these candies.

Ingredients

2 tablespoons tasteless vegetable oil, such as safflower oil, divided

1 1/2 cups whipping cream

2 cups sugar

1/3 cup honey

1/2 cup light corn syrup

2 tablespoons unsalted butter, softened

1 tablespoon instant espresso powder dissolved in 1 tablespoon water

Line an 8-inch square baking pan with aluminum foil that extends over the sides. With a paper towel coat the bottom and sides of the foil with 1 tablespoon of the vegetable oil; set aside.

In a 3-quart heavy-bottomed saucepan over medium heat, bring the cream to a boil. Add the sugar, honey, and corn syrup, and return the mixture to a boil. Wash down the sides of the pan 2 times with a pastry brush dipped in warm water, to prevent the sugar from crystallizing. Increase the heat to medium-high, place a candy thermometer in the pan, and cook the mixture until it registers 257°F on the thermometer (10 to 15 minutes), stirring occasionally.

Remove the pan from the heat; stir in the butter and dissolved espresso, then pour the mixture into the prepared pan. Let the caramel cool completely at room temperature (2 to 3 hours).

With the remaining tablespoon of vegetable oil, coat a cutting board and the blade of a large chef's knife. Remove the candy from the pan by lifting out the foil; invert the caramel onto the cutting board and peel the foil off the caramel. Cut the caramel into 8 1-inch-wide strips, then cut each strip into 8 pieces. In a tightly covered container, between sheets of waxed paper, or wrapped in waxed paper squares, the caramels will keep for 2 weeks at room temperature.

Chocolate Cashew Caramel Squares

Yield: 64 1-inch squares

Chocolate caramels with cashews are dipped in bittersweet chocolate for a very chocolaty and nutty candy. These are my husband's favorite caramel candies.

Ingredients

1 tablespoon unsalted butter, softened

2/3 cup sugar

2 tablespoons water

3/4 cup whipping cream

1 pound bittersweet chocolate, finely chopped

3/4 cup finely chopped lightly toasted cashews, plus 64 lightly toasted cashew halves

1 pound bittersweet chocolate, to be tempered (see pages 24, 29-31)

Line an 8-inch square baking pan with aluminum foil that extends over the sides. Coat the foil with the butter; set aside.

In a 2-quart heavy-bottomed saucepan over medium-high heat, combine the sugar and the water, and cook until the mixture begins to turn a rich golden brown (8 to 10 minutes). Brush down the sides of the pan with a pastry brush dipped in warm water 2 times while the mixture is cooking, to prevent the sugar from crystallizing.

In a 1-quart saucepan over medium heat, bring the cream to a boil. Immediately pour the hot cream into the caramel mixture and stir vigorously with a long-handled wooden spoon to dissolve any hard spots. Be careful when adding the cream; it will bubble vigorously.

Remove the pan from the heat and blend in the chopped chocolate in three stages until the mixture is smooth and creamy, stirring to melt the chocolate. Blend in the chopped cashews.

Immediately turn the mixture into the foil-lined pan and spread it into the corners. Cover the pan with plastic wrap and chill in the refrigerator for 2 hours, or for 30 minutes in the freezer.

Remove the candy from the pan by lifting out the foil. Invert the candy onto a cutting board and gently peel the foil off the back of the candy. With a large chef's knife, cut the candy evenly into 1-inch squares.

Melt and temper the remaining pound of chocolate. Line 2 baking sheets with parchment or waxed paper. Dip a square into the tempered chocolate, coating it completely. With a fork or dipper, remove the square from the chocolate, carefully shake off the excess chocolate, and turn the square out onto the paper. Repeat with the remaining squares. After dipping 4 squares, center a cashew half on each square before the chocolate sets up. Press lightly on the cashew so it will adhere. Let the chocolate set at room temperature or chill in the refrigerator for 15 minutes. When the caramel squares are set, place them in paper candy cups. In a tightly covered container wrapped in several layers of aluminum foil, the caramel squares will keep for 1 month in the refrigerator or 2 months in the freezer. The caramel squares are best eaten at room temperature.

Variations

Substitute milk chocolate for the bittersweet chocolate.
Substitute any nuts for the cashews.

Turtles

Yield: 60 pieces

These classic candies are pecan clusters topped with rich, creamy caramel, then dipped in chocolate. They will definitely impress your friends.

Ingredients

5 cups pecan halves

1 cup whipping cream

1/2 cup light corn syrup

1/2 cup firmly packed light brown sugar

1/3 cup granulated sugar

2 tablespoons unsalted butter, softened, cut into pieces

2 teaspoons vanilla extract

1 pound bittersweet chocolate, to be tempered (see pages 24, 29-31)

Line 2 baking sheets with aluminum foil. On the baking sheets, arrange 60 clusters of 4 pecan halves each, with 1 inch of space between the clusters. Set aside.

In a 2-quart heavy-bottomed saucepan over medium heat, combine the cream, corn syrup, brown sugar, granulated sugar, and butter. Stir until the mixture comes to a boil (5 to 8 minutes). Wash down the sides of the pan 2 times with a pastry brush dipped in warm water, to prevent the sugar from crystallizing.

Increase the heat to medium-high, place a candy thermometer in the pan, and cook the mixture until it registers 246°F on the thermometer (15 to 20 minutes), stirring constantly.

Remove the pan from the heat and stir in the vanilla. Pour the caramel into a 2-quart mixing bowl and stir to cool slightly (about 1 minute).

Spoon a tablespoon of caramel into the center of each pecan cluster. Let the caramel set completely at room temperature (about 30 minutes).

Melt and temper the chocolate. Line 2 baking sheets with parchment or waxed paper. Spoon a tablespoon of chocolate over the caramel on each turtle, or dip a turtle into the chocolate, coating it completely. With a fork or dipper, remove the turtle from the chocolate, shake off the excess chocolate, and turn the turtle out onto the paper. Repeat with the remaining turtles. Let the chocolate set at room temperature or chill in the refrigerator for 15 minutes. In a tightly covered container wrapped in several layers of aluminum foil, the candies will keep for 1 month in the refrigerator or 2 months in the freezer. They are best eaten at room temperature.

Variations

Substitute whole unblanched almonds, or walnut halves, for the pecans. Substitute milk chocolate for the bittersweet chocolate.

Nut Brittles & Marzipan

*N*uts add marvelous flavors and intriguing textures to many confections. All the candies in this chapter contain nuts, although the textures and finished candies are very different.

Several recipes for nut brittles and marzipan confections are offered here. All brittles have their basic sugar mixtures cooked to very high temperatures, so be careful when cooking them. Use a wooden spoon with a long handle for stirring. Always have all the ingredients measured out and within easy reach, and have all the equipment right at hand and ready to use. Once you begin cooking the brittle, there will be no time to search for missing ingredients or equipment.

Brittles are very susceptible to humidity and will become sticky and crumbly when exposed to too much moisture. For this reason, rainy days are not the best time to make them. Also, they should be stored at room temperature in airtight containers; moisture from the refrigerator or freezer will cause them to break down.

Marzipan has been around for centuries. It originated in the Middle East and migrated to North Africa, then to Europe. It was in Europe that the technique of using marzipan to make candies was refined. It has a sweet almond flavor and a slightly grainy texture, and can be eaten plain or flavored.

Although I emphasize making candies from scratch throughout this book, for marzipan I make an exception. Recipes in this chapter call for top-quality commercial marzipan that can be purchased in most supermarkets or specialty stores in 7-ounce rolls. Homemade marzipan prepared from the recipe on page 142 may be substituted.

When I was an apprentice at E. Rosa Salva Pasticceria in Venice, Italy, I watched the chefs make marzipan. Almonds and sugar were ground together between very heavy steel rollers that resembled the rollers used to squeeze out excess water on old-fashioned washing machines. This rolling process makes an extremely smooth marzipan, which would be difficult to duplicate at home.

Marzipan must be kept from contact with air, which causes it to dry out. If this happens, simply cut off the dry part and discard; kneading it back into the marzipan would cause undesirable changes in the texture. Tightly wrapped and sealed from exposure to the air, marzipan will keep for several months in the refrigerator or freezer.

Marzipan is fun to work with because you can get your hands into it, it's hard to make a mistake, it's very versatile, and it tastes good. Brittles are more difficult to work with, but the results are well worth the effort.

Praline

Praline is a mixture of nuts and caramelized sugar that is cooked together, cooled, and finely ground. It is used as an ingredient in many candies and confections. Hazelnuts or almonds are usually used to make praline.

Ingredients

1 tablespoon tasteless vegetable oil, such as safflower oil

1/2 cup sugar

1/4 cup water

1/2 cup toasted and skinned hazelnuts

Coat a 9-inch round cake pan with the vegetable oil and set aside. Combine the sugar and the water in a 1-quart heavy-bottomed saucepan and cook over high heat until the mixture begins to turn a light caramel color (about 8 minutes). Brush down the sides of the pan 2 times with a pastry brush dipped in warm water, to prevent the sugar from crystallizing.

When the mixture becomes caramel colored, quickly stir in the toasted hazelnuts with a wooden spoon, coating them completely with the caramel. Remove the pan from the heat, immediately turn the hazelnut mixture into the oiled cake pan, and let it cool completely (about 30 minutes).

Break the praline into pieces and pulverize to a powder in a food processor. In a tightly covered container, praline will keep for several months in the refrigerator or freezer. Bring the praline to room temperature before using.

Variation

Substitute any toasted nuts for the hazelnuts.

Praline Paste

This nut paste infuses candies with a rich hazelnut flavor and crunchy texture.

───── Ingredients ─────

1 cup toasted and skinned hazelnuts

3 tablespoons tasteless vegetable oil, such as safflower oil

Place the nuts and the vegetable oil in a food processor fitted with a steel blade. Pulse the mixture until it becomes a paste (about 2 minutes).

In a tightly covered container, praline paste will keep for 2 months in the refrigerator or 4 months in the freezer. Bring it to room temperature before using.

───── Variation ─────

Substitute any toasted nuts for the hazelnuts. When other nuts are used, this confection is called a nut butter.

Peanut Brittle

Yield: 4 1/2 cups

This version of the all-time American favorite is crisp, chewy, and very peanutty. After trying it you will probably never eat store-bought peanut brittle again.

Ingredients

2 tablespoons tasteless vegetable oil, such as safflower oil

2 cups sugar

1/2 cup water

1/2 teaspoon cream of tartar

2 cups toasted, salted peanuts

Coat a baking sheet with the vegetable oil; set aside. In a 3-quart heavy-bottomed saucepan over high heat, cook the sugar, the water, and cream of tartar until it is a medium caramel color. Brush down the sides of the pan with a pastry brush dipped in warm water 2 times, to prevent the sugar from crystallizing.

Add the peanuts and stir with a wooden spoon to coat them completely with the caramel. Remove the pan from the heat, pour the mixture onto the oiled baking sheet, and spread it out with the wooden spoon. It is necessary to work very fast, because the mixture sets up rapidly.

Let the peanut brittle cool completely (about 30 minutes), then break it into pieces with your hands. In a tightly covered container, the brittle will keep for 1 week at room temperature.

Variation

Substitute any toasted nuts for the peanuts.

Butter Peanut Brittle

Yield: 6 cups

This rendition of Peanut Brittle is enriched with butter and a dash of vanilla. The butter and baking soda make it opaque instead of clear.

Ingredients

4 tablespoons unsalted butter, divided

2 cups sugar

1/2 cup water

1 cup light corn syrup

1 teaspoon baking soda

1 teaspoon vanilla extract

2 cups toasted, salted peanuts

Coat the back of a baking sheet with 2 tablespoons of the butter; set aside. In a 3-quart heavy-bottomed saucepan over high heat, cook the sugar, the water, and corn syrup until it registers 300°F on a sugar thermometer (10 to 15 minutes). Brush down the sides of the pan with a pastry brush dipped in warm water 2 times, to prevent the sugar from crystallizing.

Remove the saucepan from the heat and with a long-handled wooden spoon rapidly stir in 1 tablespoon of the butter, the baking soda, vanilla, and peanuts. Be careful; the mixture will bubble and foam. Immediately turn the mixture onto the buttered baking sheet and spread out thin with the wooden spoon. Let the brittle cool for 5 minutes, then loosen it from the pan with a flexible-blade spatula. Butter your fingertips with the remaining tablespoon of butter, and stretch the brittle as thin as possible. Let the brittle cool completely (about 30 minutes), then break it into pieces with your hands. In a tightly covered container, the brittle will keep for 1 week at room temperature.

Variations

Substitute any toasted nuts for the peanuts.

Coconut Brittle

Substitute 2 cups lightly toasted flaked coconut and 1/4 teaspoon salt for the peanuts.

Coconut Cashew Brittle

Substitute 1 cup toasted, salted cashews and 1 cup lightly toasted flaked or ribbon coconut for the peanuts.

English Toffee

Sugar, water, butter, and chopped almonds are cooked together until they caramelize to make this rich and chewy confection. Cut into rectangular shapes, dipped in chocolate, and covered with chopped almonds, these are hard to resist.

Ingredients

3 tablespoons tasteless vegetable oil, such as safflower oil

1 1/4 cups unsalted butter

1 cup sugar

4 tablespoons water

1/2 teaspoon salt

2 1/2 cups sliced almonds, finely chopped, divided

12 ounces bittersweet chocolate, to be tempered (see pages 24, 29-31)

Coat a rolling pin, pizza wheel, and marble board or the back of a baking sheet with the vegetable oil; set aside. Cut the butter into a few pieces and melt in a 3-quart heavy-bottomed saucepan over low heat. Add the sugar, the water, and salt; increase the heat to medium and cook the mixture until it registers 260°F on a sugar thermometer (about 10 minutes), stirring constantly with a wooden spoon. Add 1/2 cup of the chopped almonds and continue cooking until the mixture becomes golden brown and registers 305°F on the thermometer (about 8 minutes), stirring constantly.

Carefully remove the pan from the heat and pour the mixture onto the oiled board. With the oiled rolling pin quickly spread out the mixture very thin. It is necessary to work fast, because the mixture sets up rapidly and becomes too brittle to cut. While still warm, with the oiled pizza wheel score the toffee into pieces that are 1 1/2 inches long and 1/2 inch wide. Let these centers set until cold (about 30 minutes).

Melt and temper the chocolate. Either dip the toffee in chocolate immediately, or store it in a tightly covered container at room temperature. If left exposed to the air, the toffee will absorb moisture and become soft.

Line 3 baking sheets with parchment or waxed paper. Sprinkle the remaining 2 cups chopped almonds on one of the paper-lined baking sheets. Dip the toffee pieces into the tempered chocolate, coating them completely, 1 piece at a time. With a dipper or fork remove the toffee from the chocolate, shake off the excess chocolate gently, and drop the toffee into the chopped almonds. Roll the toffee in the almonds, coating it thoroughly, and turn out onto the paper-lined sheets to set up completely, or chill in the refrigerator for 15 minutes. In a tightly covered container wrapped in several layers of aluminum foil, the toffee will keep for 2 months in the refrigerator.

—————— **Variation** ——————

Substitute milk chocolate for the bittersweet chocolate.

Florentines

Yield: 20 3-inch round florentines

These rich and chewy confections are an old world classic, unusual in that they are first cooked and then baked. A melange of ingredients, including honey and candied orange peel, is used to make them; their underside is covered with bittersweet chocolate.

Ingredients

3 tablespoons tasteless vegetable oil, such as safflower oil

10 tablespoons unsalted butter

2/3 cup sugar

2 tablespoons honey

1/4 cup whipping cream

2 cups sliced almonds

2/3 cup candied orange peel, finely diced (see page 184)

2 tablespoons all-purpose flour

8 ounces bittersweet chocolate, to be tempered (see pages 24, 29-31)

Position the oven racks to the upper and lower third of the oven and preheat to 350°F. Lightly oil 2 baking sheets and 20 2 1/2-inch-diameter flan rings. Place the flan rings on the baking sheets, leaving 2 inches between them.

Combine the butter, sugar, honey, and cream in a 2-quart heavy-bottomed saucepan. Cook the mixture over medium-high heat until it registers 248°F on a sugar thermometer, stirring constantly with a wooden spoon. Immediately add the almonds, candied orange peel, and flour, and stir vigorously until thoroughly blended (about 1 minute), then remove from the heat.

Place a generous tablespoon of the mixture into each oiled flan ring. Dip the back of a spoon in a bowl of cold water, shake off the excess, and press the mound in each flan ring to flatten.

Bake until golden brown (about 10 minutes), then remove the baking sheets from the oven and lift off the flan rings. Place the baking sheets on cooling racks for 5 minutes, then remove the florentines from the baking sheets using a flexible-blade spatula. If the florentines are too cold and do not release easily, return the baking sheet to the oven for 1 minute and try to remove them again. Place the florentines on cooling racks.

Melt and temper the chocolate. Line a baking sheet with parchment or waxed paper. Using a flexible-blade spatula, spread the bottom of each florentine with a tablespoon of the tempered chocolate, then with a pastry comb make a wavy pattern in the chocolate. Place the florentines on the baking sheet, chocolate side up, and place the baking sheet in the refrigerator until the chocolate is set (about 10 minutes). In a tightly covered container, between sheets of waxed paper, the florentines will keep for 1 week at room temperature.

Krokant

Yield: 100 1-inch squares or 60 1 1/2-inch circles

A relative of English toffee, Krokant is a chewy nut brittle rich with almonds, butter, and vanilla. It is eaten plain or dressed up by dipping in chocolate. It is also used to make other candies.

Ingredients

3 tablespoons tasteless vegetable oil, such as safflower oil

1 cup sugar

1/2 cup light corn syrup

3 tablespoons water

1/2 vanilla bean, split lengthwise

2 cups sliced almonds, finely chopped

1/4 teaspoon salt

4 1/2 tablespoons unsalted butter, cut into small pieces

12 ounces bittersweet chocolate, to be tempered (see pages 24, 29-31), optional

Coat the back of a baking sheet, a metal rolling pin, a 1 1/2-inch round cutter, and the blade of a large chef's knife or a pizza wheel with the vegetable oil; set aside.

In a 2-quart heavy-bottomed saucepan over high heat, bring the sugar, corn syrup, and the water to a boil. Brush down the sides of the pan with a pastry brush dipped in warm water 2 times, to prevent the sugar from crystallizing. Add the split vanilla bean and cook until the mixture registers 240°F on a sugar thermometer, stirring constantly with a wooden spoon.

Add the almonds, salt, and butter, and stir constantly until the mixture registers 290°F on a sugar thermometer. Remove the pan from the heat and immediately pour the mixture onto the oiled baking sheet. With the oiled rolling pin, roll out the mixture to 1/8 inch thick. With a fork, remove the vanilla bean. It is necessary to work very fast because the mixture sets up rapidly and becomes too brittle to cut. Cut out circles with the oiled round cutter and cut the remainder of the Krokant into 1 inch squares with the oiled chef's knife or pizza wheel.

Let the Krokant cool completely (about 30 minutes), then separate it into the circles and squares with your fingers. The remaining pieces can be ground to a fine powder in a food processor for use in other recipes. In a tightly covered container, between sheets of waxed paper, Krokant will keep for 2 weeks at room temperature.

Melt and temper the chocolate, if used. Line a baking sheet with parchment or waxed paper. Place a piece of the Krokant in the tempered chocolate, coating it completely. With a dipper or fork remove the piece from the chocolate, gently shake off the excess chocolate, and turn the Krokant out onto the paper. Repeat with the remaining pieces of Krokant. After dipping 4 pieces, press the tines of the fork onto the top of each piece to form a line design.

Let the chocolate set at room temperature or chill in the refrigerator for 15 minutes. Place the finished Krokant in paper candy cups. In a tightly covered container, the Krokant will keep for 1 week at room temperature.

Variation

Substitute toasted, skinned, and finely chopped hazelnuts for the almonds.

Nougatine

Yield: 60 1-inch squares or 40 1 1/2-inch circles

Nougatine is a crisp nut brittle made by cooking sugar with no liquid. The sugar must be stirred constantly to avoid burning or lumps from forming. Nougatine is eaten plain, dipped in chocolate, or used as an ingredient in other candies.

Ingredients

3 tablespoons tasteless vegetable oil, such as safflower oil

1 3/4 cups sugar

10 drops freshly squeezed lemon juice

1 cup lightly toasted almonds, finely chopped

12 ounces bittersweet chocolate, to be tempered (see pages 24, 29-31), optional

Coat the back of a baking sheet, a metal rolling pin, a 1 1/2-inch round cutter, and the blade of a large chef's knife or a pizza wheel with the vegetable oil; set aside.

In a 1-quart heavy-bottomed saucepan over medium-high heat, heat 1/2 cup of the sugar, stirring constantly with a wooden spoon. The sugar will become grainy, then begin to melt. When it is smooth and liquid, sprinkle on another 1/2 cup of the sugar and stir constantly until it becomes liquid. Continue in this manner with the remaining 3/4 cup sugar.

When all the sugar is melted, remove the pan from the heat and stir in the lemon juice thoroughly; add the almonds and stir vigorously to coat them completely with the caramel. Immediately pour the mixture onto the oiled baking sheet. With the oiled rolling pin, roll out the mixture to 1/8 inch thick. It is necessary to work very fast because the mixture sets up rapidly and becomes too brittle to cut. Cut out circles with the oiled round cutter and cut the remainder of the nougatine into 1-inch squares with the oiled chef's knife or a pizza wheel.

Let the nougatine cool completely (about 30 minutes), then separate it into the circles and squares with your fingers. The remaining pieces can be ground to a fine powder in a food processor for use in other recipes. In a tightly covered container, nougatine will keep for 2 weeks at room temperature.

Melt and temper the chocolate, if used. Line a baking sheet with parchment or waxed paper. Place a piece of the nougatine into the tempered chocolate, coating it completely. With a dipper or fork remove the nougatine from the chocolate, gently shake off the excess chocolate, and turn the nougatine out onto the paper. Repeat with the remaining nougatine pieces. After dipping 4 pieces, sprinkle a pinch of the ground nougatine on top of each piece.

Let the chocolate set at room temperature or chill in the refrigerator for 15 minutes. Place the finished nougatine in paper candy cups. In a tightly covered container, the nougatine will keep for 1 week at room temperature.

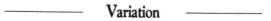

Variation

Substitute toasted, skinned, and finely chopped hazelnuts for the almonds.

Molasses Walnut Brittle

Yield: 6 cups

Molasses adds a tantalizing depth and rich taste to this crunchy brittle.

Ingredients
---

4 tablespoons unsalted butter, divided

1 1/2 cups sugar

1/2 cup water

1/4 cup molasses

1/4 cup light corn syrup

1/4 teaspoon salt

1 1/2 cups coarsely chopped walnuts, or other nuts

1/2 teaspoon baking soda

1 teaspoon vanilla extract

Coat the back of a baking sheet with 2 tablespoons of the butter; set aside. Combine the sugar, the water, molasses, and corn syrup in a 3-quart heavy-bottomed saucepan over high heat, and cook until the mixture registers 268°F on a sugar thermometer (about 10 minutes). Brush down the sides of the pan with a pastry brush dipped in warm water 2 times, to prevent the sugar from crystallizing. Add 1 tablespoon of the butter, salt, and walnuts, and cook the mixture until it registers 300°F on a sugar thermometer, stirring constantly with a wooden spoon.

Remove the saucepan from the heat and rapidly stir in the baking soda and vanilla. Be careful; the mixture will bubble and foam. Immediately turn the mixture onto the buttered baking sheet and spread out thin with the wooden spoon. Let the brittle cool for 5 minutes, then loosen it from the pan with a flexible-blade spatula. Butter your fingertips with the remaining 1 tablespoon butter and stretch the brittle as thin as possible. Let it cool completely (about 30 minutes), then break it into pieces with your hands. In a tightly covered container, the brittle will keep for 1 week at room temperature.

Hazelnut Butter Crunch Squares

Yield: 64 1-inch squares

Chocolate and hazelnuts are a classic combination. This confection is made by dipping hazelnut butter caramel into chocolate. These are my husband's favorites.

Ingredients

9 tablespoons unsalted butter, divided

1/2 cup sugar

1/8 teaspoon salt

1 tablespoon light corn syrup

1 cup toasted, skinned, and roughly chopped hazelnuts,
plus 64 whole toasted and skinned hazelnuts

1 pound bittersweet chocolate, to be tempered (see pages 24, 29-31)

Line an 8-inch square baking pan with aluminum foil, extending the foil over the sides of the pan, then coat the foil with 1 tablespoon of the butter.

In a 3-quart heavy-bottomed saucepan over medium heat, combine the remaining 8 tablespoons butter, sugar, salt, and corn syrup; stir with a wooden spoon until the mixture is smooth and liquid (about 4 minutes). Add the chopped hazelnuts and cook the mixture to a medium caramel color (5 to 8 minutes), stirring constantly. Immediately turn the mixture into the foil-lined pan and spread it into the corners. Let the candy cool completely (about 30 minutes).

Remove the candy from the pan by lifting out the foil, then gently peel the foil off the back. Cut the crunch evenly into 1-inch squares.

Melt and temper the chocolate. Line 2 baking sheets with parchment or waxed paper. Dip each square into the tempered chocolate, coating it completely. With a dipper or fork remove the square from the chocolate, carefully shake off the excess chocolate, and turn the squares out onto the paper. Repeat with the remaining squares. After dipping 4 squares, center a whole hazelnut on each square, pointed end up, before the chocolate sets up. Press lightly on the hazelnut so that it will adhere.

Let the chocolate set at room temperature or chill in the refrigerator for 15 minutes. When the squares are set, place them in paper candy cups. In a tightly covered container wrapped in several layers of aluminum foil, the squares will keep for 1 month in the refrigerator or 2 months in the freezer. These squares are best served at room temperature.

--------------- **Variations** ---------------

Substitute any nuts for the hazelnuts. These squares are also delicious without the chocolate coating.

Milk Chocolate Hazelnut Butter Crunch Squares

Substitute milk chocolate for the bittersweet chocolate.

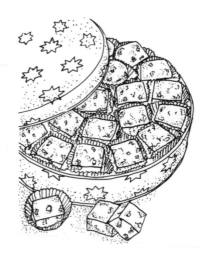

Almond Paste

Yield: 2 1/2 cups

A mixture of almonds and confectioners' sugar that have been ground together very finely, almond paste has a sweet flavor and is used as an ingredient in many candies.

Ingredients

1 1/2 cups whole blanched almonds

1 1/2 cups confectioners' sugar, or as needed, sifted

1 large egg white, lightly beaten

Combine the almonds and the 1 1/2 cups confectioners' sugar in a food processor fitted with a steel blade. Pulse the mixture until it is finely ground (about 1 minute), then add the egg white and process until the mixture forms a ball (about 30 seconds).

If the almond paste seems sticky, add more confectioners' sugar, a tablespoon at a time, until it is smooth. Tightly wrapped in plastic the almond paste will keep for 3 months in the refrigerator or 6 months in the freezer. Bring the almond paste to room temperature before using.

Variation

Substitute any nuts for the almonds. Some nuts may require a few tablespoons more confectioners' sugar to offset the stickiness caused by their higher natural oil content.

Marzipan

Yield: 1 pound

Made from almond paste but having a firmer and smoother texture, marzipan is easier to handle. It is used for decorating and as an ingredient in candies.

Ingredients

3 cups confectioners' sugar, sifted

1 recipe Almond Paste (see page 141)

2 large egg whites, lightly beaten

Dust a marble or wood board with a few tablespoons of the confectioners' sugar. Place the Almond Paste on the board and make a well in the center of the paste. Add the egg whites and 1 cup of the remaining confectioners' sugar.

Knead the mixture together, adding the remaining confectioners' sugar as needed to make a smooth and pliable texture (about 5 minutes). Marzipan should have the consistency of pie dough when completed.

Tightly wrapped in plastic, marzipan will keep for 3 months in the refrigerator or 6 months in the freezer. Bring the marzipan to room temperature before using.

Variations

Optional flavorings for Marzipan include 1 to 2 tablespoons liqueur, 1 to 2 tablespoons espresso, or 1 to 2 teaspoons extract (lemon, vanilla, orange). Knead in the flavoring with the egg whites.

Striped Marzipan Squares

Yield: 40 1-inch squares

Colored and flavored layers of marzipan are stacked one on top of another and cut into squares to create this yummy candy.

Ingredients

2 rolls (14 ounces total) marzipan

1/2 to 3/4 cup confectioners' sugar, sifted

2 teaspoons espresso coffee

2 teaspoons Grand Marnier or other orange-flavored liqueur

4 drops orange paste food color

1 large egg white, lightly beaten

Divide the marzipan into 4 equal pieces. Work with 1 piece at a time, keeping the other 3 pieces covered with plastic wrap. Dust a work surface with some of the confectioners' sugar and knead (see page 32) the espresso coffee into 1 piece of the marzipan until thoroughly blended (about 2 minutes). Add more confectioners' sugar as needed to keep the marzipan from sticking. Cover this piece of espresso marzipan with plastic wrap while working with another piece. Knead the Grand Marnier and orange paste food color into another piece of the marzipan until thoroughly blended (about 2 minutes), adding more confectioners' sugar as needed to keep the marzipan from sticking. Cover this piece of Grand Marnier marzipan while working with the other pieces.

Dust a work surface with some of the confectioners' sugar and roll out 1 piece of the natural-colored marzipan to a large rectangle (4 inches by 10 inches by 1/4 inch thick). Roll out the espresso marzipan to the same-sized rectangle as the natural marzipan. Brush the natural marzipan with some of the beaten egg white and then position the espresso marzipan on top of the natural marzipan, aligning the edges.

Dust a work surface with some of the confectioners' sugar and roll out the remaining piece of natural marzipan to the same-sized rectangle as the other pieces.

Brush the espresso marzipan with egg white, and position the natural marzipan on top of it, aligning the edges.

Dust a work surface with some of the confectioners' sugar and roll out the remaining piece of Grand Marnier marzipan to the same-sized rectangle as the other pieces. Brush the natural marzipan with egg white, and position the Grand Marnier marzipan on top of it, aligning the edges.

With a sharp knife, trim off all the edges to make them smooth and even, then cut the striped marzipan into 1-inch squares. Line a baking sheet with parchment or waxed paper. Place the marzipan squares on the paper and let them air dry at room temperature (about 1 hour).

Place each square in a paper candy cup. In a tightly covered container wrapped in several layers of aluminum foil, the squares will keep for 2 weeks in the refrigerator or 2 months in the freezer. They are best eaten at room temperature.

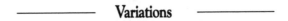

Variations

Substitute other flavors for the espresso and orange-flavored liqueur. Substitute other paste food colors for the orange to coordinate with the flavors.

Marzipan Wheels

Yield: 20 wheels

This attractive and scrumptious candy uses colored and flavored pieces of marzipan that are rolled together and then cut to form concentric multi-colored circles.

----------- **Ingredients** -----------

2 rolls (14 ounces total) marzipan

1/2 to 3/4 cup confectioners' sugar, sifted

1 tablespoon Grand Marnier or other orange-flavored liqueur

6 drops red paste food color, divided

1 large egg white, lightly beaten

Divide the marzipan into 3 equal pieces. Work with 1 piece at a time, keeping the other 2 pieces covered with plastic wrap. Dust a work surface with some of the confectioners' sugar and knead (see page 32) the Grand Marnier into the piece of the natural marzipan until thoroughly blended (about 2 minutes). Add more confectioners' sugar as needed to keep the marzipan from sticking. Cover this piece of marzipan with plastic wrap while working with the other pieces. Knead 3 drops of the red paste food color into 1 piece of the remaining marzipan until thoroughly blended (about 2 minutes), adding more confectioners' sugar as needed to keep the marzipan from sticking. Knead the remaining 3 drops red paste food color into the remaining piece of marzipan until thoroughly blended (about 2 minutes), adding more confectioners' sugar as needed to keep the marzipan from sticking.

Dust a work surface with some of the confectioners' sugar, and roll out the piece of Grand Marnier marzipan to a large rectangle (4 inches by 10 inches by 1/4 inch thick). Roll out a piece of the red marzipan to a slightly larger and thinner rectangle than the Grand Marnier marzipan. Roll the remaining piece of red marzipan into a rope shape 1/2 inch thick and 10 inches long. Place this rope alongside one long end of the Grand Marnier marzipan. Brush the side of the rope and the long edge of the Grand Marnier marzipan with some of the beaten egg white. Roll the Grand Marnier marzipan around the red marzipan rope, as tight as possible, sealing the edge with beaten egg white. Roll the remaining piece of red marzipan around the Grand Marnier marzipan, as tight as possible, sealing the edge with beaten egg white.

With a sharp knife, trim the ends, then cut the marzipan rope into 1/2-inch-thick circles. Line a baking sheet with parchment or waxed paper. Place the marzipan wheels on the paper and let them air dry at room temperature (about 1 hour).

Place each wheel in a paper candy cup. In a tightly covered container wrapped in several layers of aluminum foil, the wheels will keep for 2 weeks in the refrigerator or 2 months in the freezer. They are best eaten at room temperature.

Variation

Substitute other paste food colors for the red color. Substitute other flavors for the Grand Marnier.

Marzipan Logs

Children enjoy making these flavored marzipan logs because they are fun to eat and very easy to prepare (cooking is not necessary).

Ingredients

1/3 cup confectioners' sugar, sifted

1 roll (7 ounces) marzipan

1 teaspoon lemon extract

14 slivers candied lemon peel (see page 184)

Dust a work surface and your hands with some of the confectioners' sugar. Make a few indentations in the marzipan and add the lemon extract. Knead the marzipan (see page 32) in the confectioners' sugar to blend in the extract thoroughly (about 2 minutes).

Break off pieces of marzipan about the size of a walnut; you should have 14 pieces. Roll each piece first into a ball, then into a log about 2 1/2 inches long and 3/4 inch in diameter. Press a sliver of candied lemon peel into the center of each log and place in a paper candy cup.

In a tightly covered container wrapped in several layers of aluminum foil, the logs will keep for 2 weeks in the refrigerator. They are best served at room temperature.

Variations

For "adult" marzipan logs, substitute Frangelico, Amaretto, Grand Marnier, vanilla extract, or orange extract for the lemon extract. Substitute the decoration to match the liqueur used.

Chocolate-Dipped Marzipan Logs

Melt and temper 6 ounces bittersweet chocolate (see pages 24, 29-31). Line a baking sheet with parchment or waxed paper. Dip a marzipan log into the tempered chocolate, coating it completely. With a dipper or fork, remove the log from the chocolate, shake off the excess chocolate, and turn the log out onto the paper. After dipping 4 logs, place a sliver of candied lemon peel on top of each log before the chocolate sets up. Repeat with the remaining logs.

Let the chocolate set at room temperature or chill in the refrigerator 15 minutes. When the chocolate is set, place the logs in paper candy cups. In a tightly covered container wrapped in several layers of aluminum foil, the logs will keep for 2 weeks in the refrigerator. They are best served at room temperature.

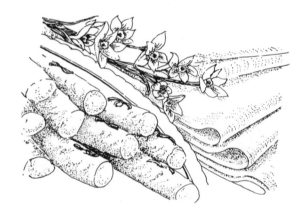

Orange Marzipan Hearts

Yield: 32 1 1/2-inch hearts

Natural marzipan is flavored with chopped candied orange peel and Grand Marnier, then cut into heart shapes.

Ingredients

1/3 cup confectioners' sugar, sifted

1 tablespoon Grand Marnier or other orange-flavored liqueur

3 tablespoons finely chopped candied orange peel (see page 184), plus 32 slivers candied orange peel

1 roll (7 ounces) marzipan

On a work surface dusted with some of the confectioners' sugar, knead (see page 32) the Grand Marnier and candied orange peel into the marzipan until thoroughly blended (about 2 minutes). Add more confectioners' sugar as needed to keep the marzipan from sticking.

Dust a work surface with some of the confectioners' sugar and roll out the marzipan to 1/4 inch thick. Line a baking sheet with parchment or waxed paper. With a 1 1/2-inch-diameter heart-shaped cutter, cut shapes out of the marzipan. After every few cuts, dip the cutter in some of the confectioners' sugar, and shake off the excess, to keep it from sticking. With a flexible-blade spatula, transfer the marzipan hearts to the paper-lined baking sheet. Press a sliver of candied orange peel into the center of each heart.

Let the hearts air dry at room temperature (about 1 hour). Place each heart in a paper candy cup. In a tightly covered container wrapped in several layers of aluminum foil, the hearts will keep for 2 weeks in the refrigerator. They are best eaten at room temperature.

Substitute any shape cutter to cut out the marzipan.

Chocolate Orange Marzipan Hearts

Cut out the marzipan hearts, transfer to the lined baking sheet, cover with plastic wrap, and refrigerate for 1 hour.

Melt and temper 12 ounces bittersweet chocolate (see pages 24, 29-31). Line a baking sheet with parchment or waxed paper. Remove the hearts from the refrigerator and place a heart in the tempered chocolate, coating completely. With a dipper or fork remove the heart from the chocolate, carefully shake off the excess chocolate, and turn the heart out onto the paper. Repeat with the remaining hearts. After dipping 4 hearts, place a sliver of candied orange peel in the center of each heart before the chocolate sets up.

Let the chocolate set at room temperature or chill in the refrigerator for 15 minutes. Place the hearts in paper candy cups. In a tightly covered container wrapped in several layers of aluminum foil, the hearts will keep for 1 month in the refrigerator. They are best eaten at room temperature.

Ginger Marzipan Hearts

Substitute finely chopped crystallized ginger for the candied orange peel.

Chocolate Ginger Marzipan Hearts

Cut out the ginger marzipan hearts, transfer to the lined baking sheet, cover with plastic wrap, and refrigerate for 1 hour. Dip the hearts in tempered bittersweet chocolate as above.

Marzipan Chocolate Squares

Yield: 72 1-inch squares

In these candies two layers of natural-colored marzipan surround a rich chocolate cream filling. They are cut into squares and dipped in chocolate for a doubly delicious flavor.

Ingredients

6 ounces bittersweet chocolate, finely chopped

1/2 cup whipping cream

1/4 to 1/2 cup confectioners' sugar, sifted

1 roll (7 ounces) marzipan

1 1/2 pounds bittersweet chocolate, to be tempered (see pages 24, 29-31)

Melt the chopped chocolate in the top of a double boiler over hot, not simmering, water, stirring frequently with a rubber spatula to ensure even melting. In a 1-quart saucepan over medium heat, bring the cream to a boil. Remove both pans from the heat, remove the top pan of the double boiler and wipe it dry, pour the cream into the chocolate, and stir together until thoroughly blended. Transfer the mixture to a bowl, cover, let cool to room temperature, and chill until thick but not stiff (2 to 3 hours).

Dust a work surface with some of the confectioners' sugar. Divide the marzipan into quarters. Roll out each piece on the work surface to a 6-inch square, and trim off the rough edges. Fit a 12-inch pastry bag with a #4 large, plain round tip and fill partway with the chocolate cream. Line a baking sheet with parchment or waxed paper. Place 2 of the marzipan squares on the paper and pipe lines of chocolate very close together on top of the marzipan squares, leaving a 1/4-inch clear border around the edges. Top each with another square of marzipan, aligning the edges evenly. Cover the marzipan squares with plastic wrap and chill in the refrigerator for 2 hours or the freezer for 45 minutes. With a sharp knife cut the 6-inch squares into 1-inch squares, then return the squares to the freezer.

Melt and temper the chocolate. Line a baking sheet with parchment or waxed paper. Remove the squares from the freezer and place one of the squares in the tempered chocolate, coating it completely. With a dipper or fork remove the square from the chocolate, carefully shake off the excess chocolate, and turn the square out onto the paper. Repeat with the remaining squares. After dipping 4 squares, press the tines of a fork into the top of each square to create a line design before the chocolate sets up.

Let the chocolate set up at room temperature or chill in the refrigerator for 15 minutes. Place the squares in paper candy cups. In a tightly covered container wrapped in several layers of aluminum foil, the squares will keep for 1 month in the refrigerator or 2 months in the freezer. They are best eaten at room temperature.

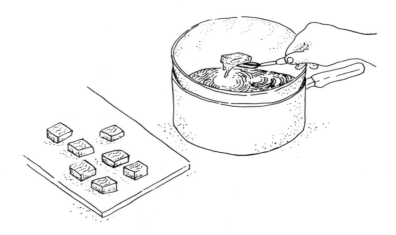

Marzipan Chocolate Rolls

Yield: 44 1/2-inch rolls

This one-bite goody has chocolate both inside and out.

Ingredients

12 ounces bittersweet chocolate, finely chopped, divided

1/2 cup whipping cream

1/4 cup confectioners' sugar, sifted

1 roll (7 ounces) marzipan

Melt 6 ounces of the chopped chocolate in the top of a double boiler over hot, not simmering, water, stirring frequently with a rubber spatula to ensure even melting. In a 1-quart saucepan over medium heat, bring the cream to a boil. Remove both pans from the heat, remove the top pan from the double boiler and wipe it dry, pour the cream into the chocolate, and stir together until thoroughly blended. Transfer the mixture to a bowl, cover, let cool to room temperature, and chill until thick but not stiff (2 to 3 hours).

Dust a work surface with some of the confectioners' sugar. Roll out the marzipan on the work surface to a 6-inch by 12-inch rectangle. With a sharp knife, trim off the rough edges and cut the marzipan in half lengthwise, forming 2 rectangles, each measuring 3 inches by 12 inches. Fit a 12-inch pastry bag with a #4 large, plain round tip and fill partway with the chocolate cream.

Line a baking sheet with parchment or waxed paper. Place each rectangle on the paper. Pipe a line of the chocolate cream lengthwise close to one side of each rectangle, leaving a 1/4 -inch clear border at each end. Moisten each lengthwise edge of the marzipan with a damp pastry brush, and roll the marzipan around the chocolate line, enclosing it completely. Cover the rolls with plastic wrap and chill in the refrigerator for 2 hours or in the freezer for 45 minutes.

Melt the remaining 6 ounces chopped chocolate in the top of a double boiler over hot, not simmering, water. Remove the marzipan rolls from the refrigerator, and with a dry pastry brush paint chocolate all over the rolls. The chocolate will firm up in a few seconds. Cut the rolls into 1/2-inch-thick slices. Place 2 rolls together in each paper candy cup.

In a tightly covered container wrapped in several layers of aluminum foil, the rolls will keep for 1 month in the refrigerator or 2 months in the freezer. They are best eaten at room temperature.

Fudge, Nougat, & Divinity

*H*omemade fudge, nougat, and divinity taste pure and fresh, unlike most store-bought varieties, which contain stabilizers and preservatives.

Using the main ingredients of sugar, butter, and cream, many different types of fudge can be made. Chocolate, coconut, coffee, and maple are some of the more popular flavors. Walnuts and almonds are the most commonly used nuts, although many other types can be used.

When making fudge several steps must be followed closely. Fudge needs to be cooked slowly over medium heat, in a heavy-bottomed saucepan. It is always cooked to the soft-ball stage (234° to 240°F) on a sugar thermometer. Then the mixture must be cooled, without stirring, to 110°F, before it is beaten. Beating the fudge evenly distributes the sugar crystals throughout the batch. This must be done after the batch has cooled, or large sugar crystals will form, resulting in a grainy-textured fudge. Beating the fudge after it has cooled causes small sugar crystals to form, which makes a smooth texture. Fudge usually tastes better if it sits for a day or two, to give the flavors time to develop.

Nougat is a popular confection in Italy and the south of France. It is often sold by vendors in open-air markets. To make nougat, a cooked sugar syrup is mixed with firmly whipped egg whites, beaten until cool, then poured into a pan and left to set for several hours. Honey or corn syrup is often used in the sugar syrup to help set the correct texture of the finished nougat by keeping the sugar from crystallizing. Like fudge, nougat is best cooked in a heavy-bottomed saucepan. It is important to monitor the temperature closely with a reliable sugar thermometer. Overcooking or undercooking the sugar syrup will make the finished nougat too firm or too soft, respectively. Try to pick a dry day to make nougat. High humidity can cause it to become too soft. Also, be sure to store nougat in a dry place. Nuts and candied fruits are usually used in nougat, and should be at room temperature before being added to the mixture. If they are cold, they will cause the nougat mixture to set too rapidly.

Nougat is usually formed in a square pan between sheets of edible rice paper. An alternate method is to line the pan with aluminum foil, which is then buttered. Nougat is easier to cut the longer it stands. Twelve hours or overnight is best. Use a sawing motion with a large chef's knife or serrated-edge knife.

Divinity is related to nougat. It is made with a cooked sugar syrup that is beaten into firmly whipped egg whites. This mixture is then beaten until cool and firm. Use a heavy-bottomed pan that conducts heat well for cooking the sugar syrup. A copper pan is perfect. As with nougat, closely monitor the temperature of the sugar syrup as it cooks. Also, like nougat, divinity is very sensitive to humidity. It should be eaten within a few days of preparation and stored in a dry place.

Chocolate Nut Fudge

Yield: *64 pieces*

This is the old-fashioned fudge remembered from childhood. It is rich and creamy with lots of chocolate and walnuts. My husband says this fudge tastes like the fudge his grandmother used to make.

Ingredients

3 tablespoons unsalted butter, softened, divided

2 cups sugar

1/4 cup light corn syrup

3/4 cup half-and-half

Pinch of salt

6 ounces bittersweet chocolate, finely chopped

1 teaspoon vanilla extract

1 1/2 cups roughly chopped walnut halves

Line an 8-inch square baking pan with aluminum foil that extends over the sides, then butter the foil with 1 tablespoon of the butter. Set aside.

In a 3-quart heavy-bottomed saucepan over medium heat, cook the sugar, corn syrup, half-and-half, and salt until the sugar is dissolved (about 5 minutes), stirring constantly with a long-handled wooden spoon. Brush down the sides of the pan with a pastry brush dipped in warm water, to prevent the sugar from crystallizing. Remove the pan from the heat and blend in the chocolate, stirring until it is completely melted and smooth (about 3 minutes).

Return the pan to the heat, place a sugar thermometer in the pan, and over medium heat bring the mixture to a boil. Cook the mixture without stirring until it registers 238°F on the thermometer. Remove the pan from the heat, remove the thermometer from the pan, and place the thermometer in warm water to cool. Sprinkle a marble board or the back of a baking sheet with cold water and immediately pour the hot mixture onto the marble. Do not scrape out the bottom of the pan. Dot the surface of the mixture with the remaining 2 tablespoons butter. Let the mixture cool on the marble until it registers 110°F on the thermometer (about 5 minutes). If using the baking sheet instead of the marble, the cooling time will be about 15 minutes.

Beat the fudge using one of the following three methods. With a 5-inch-wide flexible-blade scraper, transfer the cooled mixture to the bowl of an electric mixer, add the vanilla, and with the flat beater, beat the mixture until it thickens and loses its shine (5 to 10 minutes). Or transfer the mixture to a 2-quart mixing bowl, add the vanilla, and beat the mixture with a long-handled wooden spoon until it thickens and loses its shine (10 to 15 minutes). In both cases, add the walnuts and mix until they are blended (about 30 seconds). Or spread the mixture into a large rectangle on the marble board, sprinkle on the vanilla, then use the 5-inch-wide flexible-blade scraper to gather the mixture back to the center of the marble, folding in the edges. Repeat this process several times, until the mixture begins to thicken and lose its shine (5 to 10 minutes). Sprinkle on the walnuts and continue to work the fudge to incorporate them (about 1 minute).

Turn the fudge into the prepared pan. Use your fingertips to even the top and to press the fudge into the corners of the pan. Place the pan of fudge on a cooling rack and let it set completely at room temperature (1 to 2 hours).

Remove the fudge from the pan by lifting out the aluminum foil. Invert the fudge onto a cutting board, peel the foil off the back of the fudge, and re-invert the fudge. With a large chef's knife cut the fudge evenly into 1-inch squares. Between layers of waxed paper in a tightly covered container, the fudge will keep for 1 month in the refrigerator or 10 days at room temperature.

―――――――― Variation ――――――――

Substitute other nuts for the walnuts.

Coconut Cream Fudge

Yield: 64 pieces

I got the idea for this fudge while eating coconut on the beach in Hawaii. If you like the taste of coconut and vanilla, you will love this all-white confection.

Ingredients

9 tablespoons unsalted butter, softened, divided

3/4 cup whipping cream

1/2 cup half-and-half

3 1/2 cups sugar

Pinch of salt

2 teaspoons vanilla extract

1/2 cup plus 1 tablespoon shredded coconut

Line an 8-inch square baking pan with aluminum foil that extends over the sides, then butter the foil with 1 tablespoon of the butter. Set aside.

In a 3-quart heavy-bottomed saucepan over medium heat, cook the cream, half-and-half, sugar, salt, and the remaining 8 tablespoons butter until the sugar is dissolved and the butter is melted (about 5 minutes), stirring constantly with a long-handled wooden spoon. Bring the mixture to a boil, then brush down the sides of the pan with a pastry brush dipped in warm water, to prevent the sugar from crystallizing. Place a sugar thermometer in the pan and cook the mixture without stirring until it registers 238°F on the thermometer (about 12 minutes).

Remove the pan from the heat, remove the thermometer from the pan, and place the thermometer in warm water. Stir in the vanilla extract. Sprinkle a marble board or the back of a baking sheet with cold water, and immediately pour the hot mixture onto the marble. Do not scrape out the bottom of the pan. Let the mixture cool on the marble until it registers 110°F on the thermometer (about 5 minutes). If using the baking sheet instead of the marble, the cooling time will be about 15 minutes.

Beat the fudge using one of the following three methods. With a 5-inch-wide flexible-blade scraper, transfer the mixture to the bowl of an electric mixer, add the vanilla, and with the flat beater, beat the mixture until it thickens and loses its shine (5 to 10 minutes). Or transfer the mixture to a 2-quart mixing bowl, add the vanilla, and beat the mixture with a long-handled wooden spoon until it thickens and loses its shine (10 to 15 minutes). In both cases, add the coconut and mix until it is blended (about 30 seconds). Or spread the mixture into a large rectangle on the marble board, sprinkle on the vanilla, then use the 5-inch-wide flexible-blade scraper to gather the mixture back to the center of the marble, folding in the edges. Repeat this process several times, until the mixture begins to thicken and lose its shine (5 to 10 minutes). Sprinkle on the coconut and continue to work the fudge to incorporate it (about 1 minute).

Turn the fudge into the prepared pan. Use your fingertips to even the top and to press the fudge into the corners of the pan. Place the pan of fudge on a cooling rack and let it set completely at room temperature (1 to 2 hours).

Remove the fudge from the pan by lifting out the aluminum foil. Invert the fudge onto a cutting board, peel the foil off the back of the fudge, and re-invert the fudge. With a large chef's knife cut the fudge evenly into 1-inch squares. Between layers of waxed paper in a tightly covered container, the fudge will keep for 1 month in the refrigerator or 10 days at room temperature.

Variations

Nut Cream Fudge
Substitute 1/2 cup roughly chopped nuts for the coconut.
Praline Cream Fudge
Substitute 1/2 cup finely ground praline (see page 125) for the coconut.

Maple Pecan Fudge

Yield: 64 pieces

Maple and pecan are a fabulous flavor combination. Make sure to use
pure maple syrup for this yummy fudge.

Ingredients

4 tablespoons unsalted butter, softened, divided

3/4 cup pure maple syrup

1 1/2 cups half-and-half

3 cups sugar

3 tablespoons light corn syrup

Pinch of salt

2 teaspoons vanilla extract

1 1/2 cups roughly chopped pecan halves

Line an 8-inch square baking pan with aluminum foil that extends over the sides,
then butter the foil with 1 tablespoon of the butter. Set aside.

In a 3-quart heavy-bottomed saucepan over medium heat, cook the maple syrup,
half-and-half, sugar, corn syrup, and salt until the sugar is dissolved (about 5
minutes), stirring constantly with a long-handled wooden spoon. Bring the mixture
to a boil, then brush down the sides of the pan with a pastry brush dipped in warm
water, to prevent the sugar from crystallizing. Place a sugar thermometer in the pan
and cook the mixture without stirring until it registers 238°F on the thermometer
(about 12 minutes).

Remove the pan from the heat, remove the thermometer from the pan, and place
the thermometer in warm water. Sprinkle a marble board or the back of a baking sheet
with cold water and immediately pour the hot mixture onto the marble. Do not scrape
out the bottom of the pan. Dot the surface of the mixture with the remaining 3
tablespoons butter. Let the mixture cool on the marble until it registers 110°F on the
thermometer (about 5 minutes). If using the baking sheet instead of the marble, the

cooling time will be about 15 minutes.

Beat the fudge using one of the following three methods. With a 5-inch-wide flexible-blade scraper, transfer the mixture to the bowl of an electric mixer, add the vanilla, and with the flat beater, beat the mixture until it thickens and loses its shine (5 to 10 minutes). Or transfer the mixture to a 2-quart mixing bowl, add the vanilla, and beat the mixture with a long-handled wooden spoon until it thickens and loses its shine (10 to 15 minutes). In both cases, add the chopped pecans and mix until they are blended (about 30 seconds). Or spread the mixture into a large rectangle on the marble board, sprinkle on the vanilla, then use the 5-inch-wide flexible-blade scraper to gather the mixture back to the center of the marble, folding in the edges. Repeat this process several times, until the mixture begins to thicken and lose its shine (5 to 10 minutes). Sprinkle on the chopped pecans and continue to work the fudge to incorporate it (about 1 minute).

Turn the fudge into the prepared pan. Use your fingertips to even the top and to press the fudge into the corners of the pan. Place the pan of fudge on a cooling rack and let it set completely at room temperature (1 to 2 hours).

Remove the fudge from the pan by lifting out the aluminum foil. Invert the fudge onto a cutting board, peel the foil off the back of the fudge, and re-invert the fudge. With a large chef's knife cut the fudge evenly into 1-inch squares. Between layers of waxed paper in a tightly covered container, the fudge will keep for 1 month in the refrigerator or 10 days at room temperature.

———————— **Variation** ————————

Maple Walnut Fudge
Substitute walnuts for the pecans.

Espresso Hazelnut Fudge

Yield: 64 pieces

If you like cappuccino, you will love this fudge. It goes perfectly with after-dinner coffee.

Ingredients

2 1/2 tablespoons unsalted butter, softened, divided

3 tablespoons instant espresso powder dissolved in 1 1/2 cups water

3 cups sugar

1 1/2 cups whipping cream

1/4 teaspoon salt

1/2 teaspoon cream of tartar

1/2 teaspoon ground cinnamon

1 1/2 cups roughly chopped toasted hazelnuts

Line an 8-inch square baking pan with aluminum foil that extends over the sides, then butter the foil with 1 tablespoon of the butter. Set aside.

In a 3-quart heavy-bottomed saucepan over medium heat, cook the espresso, sugar, the remaining 1 1/2 tablespoons butter, cream, salt, and cream of tartar until the sugar is dissolved (about 5 minutes), stirring constantly with a long-handled wooden spoon. Bring the mixture to a boil, then brush down the sides of the pan with a pastry brush dipped in warm water, to prevent the sugar from crystallizing. Place a sugar thermometer in the pan and cook the mixture without stirring until it registers 238°F on the thermometer (about 10 minutes).

Remove the pan from the heat, remove the thermometer from the pan, and place the thermometer in warm water. Sprinkle a marble board or the back of a baking sheet with cold water and immediately pour the hot mixture onto the marble. Do not scrape out the bottom of the pan. Let the mixture cool on the marble until it registers 110°F on the thermometer (about 5 minutes). If using the baking sheet instead of the marble, the cooling time will be about 15 minutes.

Beat the fudge using one of the following three methods. With a 5-inch-wide flexible-blade scraper, transfer the mixture to the bowl of an electric mixer, add the ground cinnamon, and with the flat beater, beat the mixture until it thickens and loses its shine (5 to 10 minutes). Or transfer the mixture to a 2-quart mixing bowl, add the ground cinnamon, and beat the mixture with a long-handled wooden spoon until it thickens and loses its shine (10 to 15 minutes). In both cases, add the chopped hazelnuts and mix until they are blended (about 30 seconds). Or spread the mixture into a large rectangle on the marble board, sprinkle on the ground cinnamon, then use the 5-inch-wide flexible-blade scraper to gather the mixture back to the center of the marble, folding in the edges. Repeat this process several times, until the mixture begins to thicken and lose its shine (5 to 10 minutes). Sprinkle on the chopped hazelnuts and continue to work the fudge to incorporate it (about 1 minute).

Turn the fudge into the prepared pan. Use your fingertips to even the top and to press the fudge into the corners of the pan. Place the pan of fudge on a cooling rack and let it set completely at room temperature (1 to 2 hours).

Remove the fudge from the pan by lifting out the aluminum foil. Invert the fudge onto a cutting board, peel the foil off the back of the fudge, and re-invert the fudge. With a large chef's knife cut the fudge evenly into 1-inch squares. Between layers of waxed paper in a tightly covered container, the fudge will keep for 1 month in the refrigerator or 10 days at room temperature.

--------------- **Variation** ---------------

Espresso Almond Fudge
Substitute unblanched toasted almonds for the hazelnuts.

Almond Orange Nougat

Yield: 64 pieces

This classic nougat is chock-full of almonds and candied orange peel. After you try it, you will doubtless never eat store-bought nougat again.

Ingredients

3 tablespoons unsalted butter, softened, divided

1 1/2 cups light corn syrup

2 cups sugar

1/4 cup water

Pinch of salt

2 large egg whites, at room temperature

Pinch of cream of tartar

1/2 teaspoon vanilla extract

1 1/2 teaspoons almond extract

1 cup roughly chopped toasted whole almonds

1/2 cup finely diced candied orange peel (see page 184)

1 pound bittersweet chocolate, to be tempered (see pages 24, 29-31)

Line an 8-inch square baking pan with aluminum foil that extends over the sides. Cut another square of foil to fit the top of the pan. Butter the foil in the pan and the foil square with 1 tablespoon of the butter. Set the pan aside.

In a 3-quart heavy-bottomed saucepan over medium heat, cook the corn syrup, sugar, the water, and salt until the sugar is dissolved (about 5 minutes), stirring constantly with a long-handled wooden spoon. Brush down the sides of the pan with a pastry brush dipped in warm water, to prevent the sugar from crystallizing. Increase the heat to medium-high, place a sugar thermometer in the pan, and cook the mixture without stirring until it registers 250°F on the thermometer (about 10 minutes).

Brush down the sides of the pan with a pastry brush dipped in water 2 more times during the cooking process.

While the mixture is cooking, in the bowl of an electric mixer with a wire whip, beat the egg whites on medium speed until they are frothy. Add the cream of tartar, increase the speed to medium-high, and beat the egg whites until they hold firm peaks (3 to 5 minutes).

Remove the pan with the sugar syrup from the heat, and pour one quarter of the syrup into a glass measuring cup. With the mixer at medium speed, pour the sugar syrup slowly into the beaten egg whites, and beat until the mixture is firm (about 3 minutes). Return the pan to the heat and cook the remaining sugar syrup, without stirring, to 300° F on the thermometer (about 10 minutes). With the mixer on medium speed, slowly pour the remaining hot sugar syrup into the egg whites, being careful not to drip the syrup down the sides of the bowl. Increase the mixer speed to high and beat until the mixture is cool (about 15 minutes). Blend in the vanilla and almond extracts, beat in the remaining 2 tablespoons butter, then blend in the chopped almonds and candied orange peel.

Turn the mixture into the prepared pan. Spread it out smoothly and evenly into the corners of the pan. Place the second square of buttered aluminum foil on top of the candy. Let the nougat set completely at room temperature (12 hours or overnight).

Remove the top piece of foil from the candy, then remove the candy from the pan by lifting out the foil. Invert the candy onto a cutting board, peel the foil off the back of the candy, then re-invert so the top side is facing up. With a large chef's knife dipped in hot water and dried, cut the candy into 1 inch squares using a sawing motion.

Melt and temper the bittersweet chocolate. Line 2 baking sheets with parchment or waxed paper. Dip a piece of the nougat into the tempered chocolate, coating it completely. With a fork or dipper, remove the piece from the chocolate, carefully shake off the excess chocolate, and turn the piece out onto the paper. Repeat with the remaining pieces. Let the chocolate set at room temperature, or chill in the refrigerator for 15 minutes. When the chocolate is set, place each piece in a paper candy cup. Between layers of waxed paper, in a tightly covered container wrapped in several layers of aluminum foil, the nougat will keep for 1 month in the refrigerator. The nougat is best eaten at room temperature.

Substitute other nuts for the almonds.

Almond Lemon Nougat

Substitute candied lemon peel (see candied orange peel, page 184) for the candied orange peel, and substitute lemon extract for the vanilla extract.

Almond Lime Nougat

Substitute candied lime peel (see candied orange peel, page 184) for the candied orange peel, and substitute almond extract for the vanilla extract.

Almond Tangerine Nougat

Substitute candied tangerine peel (see candied orange peel, page 184) for the candied orange peel, and substitute almond extract for the vanilla extract.

Torrone

Yield: 64 pieces

Torrone is the Italian version of nougat. The origin of torrone is uncertain, but legend has it that it was served in Cremona, Italy, during the reign of Francesco Sforza, in the fifteenth century. Torrone is full of almonds, hazelnuts, pistachio nuts, and honey.

——— Ingredients ———

2 sheets edible rice paper (8 inches by 11 inches), available at candy supply shops

3 tablespoons light corn syrup

1/2 cup honey

1 cup sugar

1/2 cup water

2 large egg whites, at room temperature

Pinch of cream of tartar

1 teaspoon vanilla extract

1 cup roughly chopped toasted sliced almonds

1 cup roughly chopped toasted and skinned hazelnuts

1 cup roughly chopped toasted pistachio nuts

Line an 8-inch square baking pan with 1 sheet of the edible rice paper, extending the paper up the sides of the pan; set aside.

In a 3-quart heavy-bottomed saucepan over medium heat, cook the corn syrup, honey, sugar, and the water until the sugar is dissolved (about 5 minutes), stirring constantly with a long-handled wooden spoon. Brush down the sides of the pan with a pastry brush dipped in warm water, to prevent the sugar from crystallizing. Increase the heat to medium-high, place a sugar thermometer in the pan, and cook the mixture, without stirring, until it registers 290°F on the thermometer (about 15 minutes). Brush down the sides of the pan with a pastry brush dipped in water 2 more times during the cooking process.

While the sugar syrup is cooking, in the bowl of an electric mixer with a wire whip, beat the egg whites on medium speed until they are frothy. Add the cream of tartar, increase the speed to medium-high, and beat the egg whites until they hold firm peaks (3 to 5 minutes).

Remove the pan with the sugar syrup from the heat, remove the thermometer from the pan, and place the thermometer in warm water to cool. With the mixer speed at medium, slowly pour the hot sugar syrup into the egg whites, being careful not to drip the sugar syrup down the sides of the bowl. Increase the mixer speed to high, and beat until the mixture is stiff (about 5 minutes). Blend in the vanilla and all the nuts.

Turn the mixture into the paper-lined pan, spreading it out smoothly and evenly into the corners of the pan. Place another sheet of rice paper on top of the candy. Place a cutting board or plate on top of the rice paper and weight it with a heavy item, such as a heavy pan. Let the torrone set for 12 hours at room temperature.

With a sharp, thin-bladed knife, release the edges of the candy from the pan. Invert the candy onto a cutting board, then re-invert, so the top side is facing up. With a serrated-edge knife, cut the candy into 1 inch squares. Between sheets of waxed paper in a tightly covered container, the candy will keep for 1 week at room temperature or 3 weeks in the refrigerator.

 Variation

Substitute walnuts or cashews for the almonds and hazelnuts.

Chocolate Hazelnut Nougat

Yield: 56 pieces

This chocolate nougat has a pronounced honey flavor. It is soft and chewy, with a slight crunchy texture from the hazelnuts.

Ingredients

1 tablespoon unsalted butter, softened

3/4 cup honey

4 ounces bittersweet chocolate, finely chopped

3 tablespoons light corn syrup

1 cup sugar

2 tablespoons water

1 large egg white, at room temperature

Pinch of cream of tartar

1 1/3 cups roughly chopped toasted and skinned hazelnuts

1/4 cup confectioners' sugar

Line a baking sheet with aluminum foil, then place a 14-inch by 4 1/2-inch flan ring in the center of the foil. Butter the foil and the inside of the flan ring with the butter; set aside. In a 1-quart saucepan over low heat, heat the honey until it is lukewarm (3 to 5 minutes). Remove the pan from the heat and cover it to keep the honey warm. In the top of a double boiler over hot, not simmering, water, melt the chocolate, stirring frequently with a rubber spatula to ensure even melting.

In a 3-quart heavy-bottomed saucepan over medium heat, cook the corn syrup, sugar, and the water until the sugar is dissolved (about 5 minutes), stirring constantly with a long-handled wooden spoon. Brush down the sides of the pan with a pastry brush dipped in warm water, to prevent the sugar from crystallizing. Increase the heat to medium-high, place a sugar thermometer in the pan, and cook the mixture without stirring until it registers 268°F on the thermometer (about 10 minutes). Brush down the sides of the pan with a pastry brush dipped in warm water 2 more times during the cooking process.

While the sugar is cooking, in the bowl of an electric mixer with a wire whip, beat the egg white on medium speed until it is frothy. Add the cream of tartar, increase the speed to medium-high, and beat the egg white until it holds firm peaks (about 3 minutes). Remove the pan with the sugar syrup from the heat, remove the thermometer from the pan, and place the thermometer in warm water to cool. Blend the beaten egg white into the sugar syrup, stirring constantly, then blend in the warm honey. Return the saucepan to low heat and cook the mixture until it thickens (about 15 minutes), stirring constantly. Remove the saucepan from the heat and blend in the melted chocolate and the chopped hazelnuts. Turn the mixture into the flan ring, spreading it out smoothly and evenly into the corners of the ring. Cover with plastic wrap and chill in the refrigerator for 1 hour, then let the nougat sit at room temperature for 12 hours.

With a sharp, thin-bladed knife, loosen and remove the flan ring from the candy. Dust a cutting board with the confectioners' sugar, invert the candy onto the cutting board, and peel the foil off the back of the candy. With a large chef's knife, cut the candy into 1-inch-wide strips across the width. Cut each strip into 4 pieces.

Between sheets of waxed paper in a tightly covered container, the candy will keep for 1 week at room temperature or 3 weeks in the refrigerator. The nougat squares are best eaten at room temperature.

--------- **Variations** ---------

Substitute other nuts for the hazelnuts.
Double Chocolate Hazelnut Nougat

Melt and temper 1 1/2 pounds bittersweet chocolate (see pages 24, 29-31). Line 2 baking sheets with parchment or waxed paper. Dip a square of the nougat into the tempered chocolate, coating it completely. With a fork or dipper, remove the square from the chocolate, carefully shake off the excess chocolate, and turn the square out onto the paper. After dipping 4 squares, touch the top of each square with the tines of the fork, making a design. Repeat with the remaining squares. Let the chocolate set at room temperature, or chill in the refrigerator for 15 minutes. When the chocolate is set, place each nougat square in a paper candy cup. In a tightly covered container wrapped in several layers of aluminum foil, the squares will keep for 1 month in the refrigerator. The nougat squares are best eaten at room temperature.

Praline Nougat

Yield: 56 pieces

This chocolate-dipped nougat combines praline paste and hazelnuts. It is always a winner, especially with chocolate lovers.

Ingredients

1 tablespoon unsalted butter, softened

1 1/4 cups granulated sugar

3/4 cup firmly packed light brown sugar

1 cup light corn syrup

1/3 cup water

1 large egg white, at room temperature

Pinch of cream of tartar

1 1/4 cups praline paste (see page 126)

1/2 cup roughly chopped, toasted and skinned hazelnuts

2 teaspoons vanilla extract

1 1/2 pounds bittersweet chocolate, to be tempered (see pages 24, 29-31)

Line a baking sheet with aluminum foil, then place a 14-inch by 4 1/2-inch flan ring in the center of the foil. Butter the foil and the inside of the flan ring with the butter; set aside

In a 3-quart heavy-bottomed saucepan over medium heat, cook the granulated sugar, brown sugar, corn syrup, and the water until the sugar is dissolved (about 5 minutes), stirring constantly with a long-handled wooden spoon. Brush down the sides of the pan with a pastry brush dipped in warm water, to prevent the sugar from crystallizing. Increase the heat to medium-high, place a sugar thermometer in the pan, and cook the mixture without stirring until it registers 246°F on the thermometer (10 to 15 minutes). Brush down the sides of the pan with a pastry brush dipped in warm water 2 more times during the cooking process.

While the sugar is cooking, in the bowl of an electric mixer with a wire whip, beat the egg white on medium speed until it is frothy. Add the cream of tartar, increase the speed to medium-high, and beat the egg white until it holds firm peaks (about 3 minutes).

Remove the pan with the sugar syrup from the heat, remove the thermometer from the pan, and place the thermometer in warm water. With the mixer on medium speed, slowly pour the sugar syrup into the beaten egg white, being careful not to drip the syrup down the sides of the bowl, and beat until the mixture is firm (about 3 minutes).

Replace the wire whip with the flat beater, set the mixer at low speed, and blend in the praline paste, hazelnuts, and vanilla, occasionally stopping to scrape down the flat beater and the sides of the bowl. Turn the mixture into the flan ring, spreading it out smoothly and evenly into the corners. Cover the nougat with plastic wrap and chill in the refrigerator for 1 hour, then let the nougat set at room temperature for 12 hours.

With a sharp, thin-bladed knife, loosen and remove the flan ring from the candy. Invert the candy onto a cutting board, and peel the foil off the back of the candy. With a large chef's knife, cut the candy into 1-inch-wide strips across the width. Cut each strip into 4 pieces.

Melt and temper the bittersweet chocolate. Line 2 baking sheets with parchment or waxed paper. Dip a piece of the nougat into the tempered chocolate, coating it completely. With a fork or dipper, remove the piece from the chocolate, carefully shake off the excess chocolate, and turn the piece out onto the paper. Repeat with the remaining nougat pieces. Let the chocolate set at room temperature, or chill in the refrigerator for 15 minutes. When the chocolate is set, place each piece in a paper candy cup. Between layers of waxed paper, in a tightly covered container wrapped in several layers of aluminum foil, the nougat will keep for 1 month in the refrigerator. The nougat is best eaten at room temperature.

——————— **Variations** ———————

Almond Butter Nougat

Substitute almond butter (see praline paste, page 126) for the praline paste, and substitute chopped whole almonds for the hazelnuts. Substitute 1 teaspoon almond extract for 1 teaspoon of the vanilla extract.

Cashew Butter Nougat

Substitute cashew butter (see praline paste, page 126) for the praline paste, and substitute chopped cashews for the hazelnuts.

Walnut Butter Nougat

Substitute walnut butter (see praline paste, page 126) for the praline paste, and substitute chopped walnut halves for the hazelnuts.

Macadamia Nut Butter Nougat

Substitute macadamia nut butter (see praline paste, page 126) for the praline paste, and substitute chopped whole macadamia nuts for the hazelnuts.

Divinity

Yield: 50 pieces

Lighter than air, these sweet puffs of divinity will melt in your mouth.

Ingredients

2 1/2 cups sugar

1/2 cup water

1/2 cup light corn syrup

2 large egg whites, at room temperature

Pinch of cream of tartar

1 cup finely chopped walnuts

1 1/2 teaspoons vanilla extract

In a 2-quart heavy-bottomed saucepan over medium heat, cook the sugar, the water, and corn syrup until the sugar is dissolved (about 5 minutes), stirring constantly with a long-handled wooden spoon. Brush down the sides of the pan with a pastry brush dipped in warm water, to prevent the sugar from crystallizing. Increase the heat to medium-high, place a sugar thermometer in the pan, and cook the mixture without stirring until it registers 256°F on the thermometer (about 10 minutes). Brush down the sides of the pan with a pastry brush dipped in warm water 2 more times during the cooking process.

While the mixture is cooking, in the bowl of an electric mixer with a wire whip, beat the egg whites on medium speed until they are frothy. Add the cream of tartar, increase the speed to medium-high, and beat the egg whites until they hold firm peaks (3 to 5 minutes).

Remove the pan with the sugar syrup from the heat. Reduce the mixer speed to medium and pour the sugar syrup slowly into the egg whites, being careful not to drip the sugar syrup down the sides of the bowl. Increase the mixer speed to high and beat until the mixture is firm and no longer shiny (10 to 15 minutes). Blend in the chopped walnuts and vanilla extract.

Line 2 baking sheets with waxed paper. Drop 1 1/2-inch-wide spoonfuls of the mixture onto the paper, leaving 1 inch between them. Let the candy set at room temperature until firm (about 30 minutes). In a tightly covered container between sheets of waxed paper, the candy will keep 4 days at room temperature.

─────────── **Variations** ───────────

Substitute other nuts for the walnuts. Black walnuts are especially good in divinity.

Praline Divinity

Substitute praline (see page 125) for the walnuts.

Seafoam Divinity

Substitute firmly packed light brown sugar for the granulated sugar. Reduce the corn syrup to 1 tablespoon, and add 2 teaspoons distilled white vinegar.

Orange Divinity

Substitute finely chopped candied orange peel (see page 184) for the finely chopped nuts, and substitute orange extract for the vanilla extract.

Lemon Divinity

Substitute finely chopped candied lemon peel (see page 184) for the finely chopped nuts, and substitute lemon extract for the vanilla extract.

Ginger Divinity

Substitute 1/3 cup finely chopped crystallized ginger for the finely chopped nuts, and substitute finely ground ginger for the vanilla extract.

Chocolate Divinity

Add 6 ounces melted bittersweet chocolate when adding the nuts.

Fruit
Candies

The primary ingredient in fruit candies is the fruit itself—either fresh, dried, or made into jam. Sugar is added to heighten the fruit's flavor and intensify its natural sweetness. Fruit candies have very little fat, which makes them ideal for people on a fat-restricted diet. These light, refreshing treats are perfect to serve after a hearty meal.

When making fresh fruit candies, whether the fruit is puréed, candied, or simply dipped in chocolate, only the best-quality fruit should be used. Always choose ripe, unblemished fruit. The best way to select fruit is to smell it. If the fruit lacks aroma, it won't have good flavor. Use the fruit shortly after buying it for the best results.

Dried fruits can also be used to create delicious and appealing candies. Dried fruits can be enhanced with honey, coconut, or flavored marzipan, or can be dipped in chocolate.

As with fresh fruit, it is important to choose dried fruit with care. Make sure that it is plump and moist. If it looks too leathery, it is too dried out, and won't provide the correct texture to your candies. Not all dried fruit is sweet, so try to sample the fruit before buying.

To ensure success when making fruit candies, closely follow the instructions given in each recipe. When a recipe calls for a mixture to be cooked to a specific temperature on the sugar thermometer, this temperature must be reached. If the mixture is cooked to too low or too high a temperature, it will not have the proper consistency.

Fruit candies are a scrumptious way to dress up a party with a variety of flavors and colors. They are delicious eaten on their own or mixed with an assortment of other candies.

Chocolate-Dipped Strawberries

Yield: 2 pints

How can you make nature's jewels even more perfect? Dip them in chocolate!

---------- **Ingredients** ----------

2 pints large or long-stemmed fresh strawberries

1 pound bittersweet or white chocolate, to be tempered (see pages 24, 29-31)

Rinse the strawberries and let dry completely on paper towels. Line 2 baking sheets with parchment or waxed paper. Melt and temper the chocolate.

Hold a strawberry securely between your thumb and forefinger, and with the pointed end down, dip the berry into the chocolate, covering three quarters of the berry. Remove the berry from the chocolate, gently shake off the excess chocolate, and place the berry on the paper. Repeat with the remaining berries. Let the chocolate set at room temperature or chill in the refrigerator for 15 minutes. The dipped berries must be served within 4 hours of preparation, either immediately or refrigerated until 15 minutes before serving.

Chocolate-Dipped Apricots

Yield: 50 pieces

Apricot and chocolate are a superb combination of flavors. This fruit confection makes an attractive presentation.

Ingredients

50 large dried apricot halves

12 ounces bittersweet or white chocolate, to be tempered (see pages 24, 29-31)

Line 2 baking sheets with parchment or waxed paper. Melt and temper the chocolate.

Hold an apricot half securely between your thumb and forefinger, and dip it halfway into the chocolate. Remove the apricot half from the chocolate, gently shake off the excess chocolate, and place the apricot half on the paper. Repeat with the remaining apricot halves. Let the chocolate set at room temperature or chill in the refrigerator for 15 minutes. Between layers of waxed paper, in a tightly covered container wrapped in several layers of aluminum foil, the apricot halves will keep for 2 weeks in the refrigerator. They are best eaten at room temperature.

Variations

Substitute dried peaches or dried pears for the apricots. Dip these into the chocolate on the diagonal for an interesting design.

Apricot-Date Balls

Yield: 40 pieces

Dried apricots and dates are mixed with honey, shaped into balls, and rolled in coconut to make a chewy, delectable confection.

Ingredients

2 cups dried apricots

2 cups dates, pitted

2 tablespoons honey

1 cup shredded coconut

Finely chop the apricots and dates, then combine in a 2-quart mixing bowl. Add the honey and blend thoroughly into the mixture. Line a baking sheet with parchment or waxed paper. Place the coconut in a round cake pan. Spoon out teaspoonfuls of the apricot-date mixture and roll into balls in your hands. Then roll the balls in the coconut, coating them completely. Place each ball in a paper candy cup. Between layers of waxed paper in a tightly covered container, the balls will keep for 3 weeks in the refrigerator. They are best eaten at room temperature.

Variations

Substitute dried peaches, dried pears, or raisins for the apricots.

Stuffed Dates

Yield: 36 dates

Dates stuffed with marzipan are an exotic confection of Middle Eastern origin. They are a snap to prepare.

Ingredients

36 large dates, pitted

2 tablespoons confectioners' sugar

1 tablespoon Grand Marnier or other orange-flavored liqueur, or

1 teaspoon orange extract

1 1/2 rolls (10 ounces total) marzipan

Line a baking sheet with aluminum foil or waxed paper. Place the dates on the baking sheet and set aside briefly.

Dust a work surface with some of the confectioners' sugar. On this surface knead (see page 32) the Grand Marnier and orange extract thoroughly into the marzipan, adding more confectioners' sugar as needed to keep the marzipan from sticking.

Break off a piece of the marzipan the size of a walnut; roll into a ball, then into a log shape. Stuff the marzipan into the center of a pitted date. Repeat with the remaining marzipan and dates. Place each date in a paper candy cup and cover the dates completely with plastic wrap. In a tightly covered container, the dates will keep for 2 weeks in the refrigerator or 5 days at room temperature. They are best eaten at room temperature.

Variations

Add 3 drops of red, orange, or green paste food color to the marzipan when kneading in the Grand Marnier and orange extract.

Substitute other liqueurs for the Grand Marnier or other extracts for the orange extract.

Stuffed Walnuts

Substitute 72 walnut halves for the dates. Press a walnut half on each side of the piece of marzipan.

Stuffed Almonds

Substitute 72 whole unblanched almonds for the dates. Press an almond on each side of the piece of marzipan.

Candied Orange Peel

Yield: 6 cups

A popular ingredient in many confections, candied orange peel is also delicious eaten plain or dipped in chocolate.

Ingredients

6 to 8 large, thick-skinned oranges

6 cups sugar, divided

1/4 cup Grand Marnier or other orange-flavored liqueur

Slice the ends off the oranges and discard. Cut the oranges into quarters, cut off all but 1/2 inch of the pulp, then cut the quarters into thin slices.

Place the orange slices in a 6-quart saucepan and cover them with cold water. Over medium-high heat, bring the water to a boil and boil for 5 minutes. Drain off the water and repeat this process with fresh cold water 2 more times.

After the third boil, drain the orange slices, rinse them in cold water, and remove any pulp that is still attached. In the saucepan combine the orange slices, 3 cups of the sugar, and the orange liqueur, and cook over low heat until the sugar is dissolved (about 5 minutes), stirring continually. Continue to cook over low heat for 1 1/2 hours, stirring frequently. Most of the sugar will be absorbed by the peel as it cooks. Remove the saucepan from the heat, and immediately begin the next step.

Place the remaining 3 cups sugar on a sheet of waxed paper. Roll spoonfuls of the orange slices in the sugar, separating the slices to coat them completely. Transfer the slices onto another sheet of waxed paper and let them air dry (20 to 30 minutes).

In a tightly covered container, the peel will keep for 2 to 3 months in the refrigerator.

Variations

Substitute 12 large lemons, 14 limes, 12 tangerines, or 4 grapefruits for the oranges.

Chocolate-Dipped Candied Orange Peel

Melt and temper 1 1/2 pounds of bittersweet chocolate (see pages 24, 29-31). Line 2 baking sheets with parchment or waxed paper. Dip a slice of the candied peel into the chocolate either completely, halfway, or on each end, thoroughly coating it. With a fork or dipper, remove the slice from the chocolate, gently shake off the excess chocolate, and turn the slice out onto the paper. Repeat with the remaining slices. Let the chocolate on the slices set at room temperature or chill in the refrigerator for 15 minutes. Place 2 slices of the finished chocolate-dipped peel in a paper candy cup. In a tightly covered container wrapped in several layers of aluminum foil, the chocolate-dipped peel will keep for 1 month in the refrigerator or 2 months in the freezer. It is best eaten at room temperature.

Raspberry-Almond Squares

Yield: 64 1-inch squares

Raspberry jam is the core of these delightful candies.

---------------------- **Ingredients** ----------------------

1 tablespoon tasteless vegetable oil, such as safflower oil

1 3/4 cups raspberry jam

1/2 cup unsweetened applesauce

3/4 cup sugar

1 teaspoon lemon extract

2/3 cup finely chopped almonds, plus 64 whole unblanched almonds

12 ounces bittersweet chocolate, to be tempered (see pages 24, 29-31)

Line an 8-inch square baking pan with plastic wrap that extends over the sides, then coat the plastic wrap with the vegetable oil; set aside.

In a 2-quart heavy-bottomed saucepan over medium-high heat, cook the jam, applesauce, and sugar until the mixture registers 240°F on a sugar thermometer (about 15 minutes), stirring constantly. Immediately remove the pan from the heat, stir in the lemon extract and chopped almonds, and turn the mixture into the prepared pan. Press the whole almonds on the top of the candy, in evenly spaced rows of 8 across in each direction. Let the candy cool completely at room temperature (about 45 minutes).

Remove the candy from the pan by lifting out the plastic wrap. Invert the candy onto a cutting board, peel the plastic wrap off the back of the candy, and re-invert the candy so that the nut side is up. With a large chef's knife, and using the whole almonds as a guide, cut the candy evenly into 1-inch squares.

Melt and temper the chocolate. Line 2 baking sheets with parchment or waxed paper. Holding a square by the top half, dip the bottom and sides of the square into the chocolate, leaving the top exposed. Remove the square from the chocolate, carefully shake off the excess chocolate, and place the square onto the paper. Repeat with the remaining squares. Let the chocolate set at room temperature, or chill in the refrigerator for 15 minutes. Place each square in a paper candy cup. Between layers of waxed paper, in a tightly covered container wrapped in several layers of aluminum foil, the squares will keep for 2 weeks in the refrigerator. They are best eaten at room temperature.

Variations

Substitute blackberry jam or strawberry jam for the raspberry jam. Substitute other nuts for the almonds.

Orange Marmalade Pecan Squares

Yield: 64 1-inch squares

This tangy and chewy candy uses pecans and a generous amount of orange marmalade.

Ingredients

1 tablespoon tasteless vegetable oil, such as safflower oil

2 cups orange marmalade

1/2 cup unsweetened applesauce

1 3/4 cups sugar

2 teaspoons Grand Marnier or other orange-flavored liqueur

2/3 cup finely chopped pecans, plus 64 pecan halves

Line an 8-inch square baking pan with plastic wrap that extends over the sides, then coat the plastic wrap with the vegetable oil. In a 2-quart heavy-bottomed saucepan over medium-high heat, cook the jam, applesauce, and sugar until the mixture registers 250°F on a sugar thermometer (15 to 20 minutes), stirring constantly. Immediately remove the pan from the heat, stir in the Grand Marnier and the chopped pecans, and turn the mixture into the prepared pan. Press the pecan halves on the top of the candy in evenly spaced rows of 8 across in each direction. Let the candy cool completely at room temperature (about 45 minutes).

Remove the candy from the pan by lifting out the plastic wrap. Invert the candy onto a cutting board, peel the plastic wrap off the back of the candy, and re-invert the candy so that the nut side is up. With a large chef's knife, and using the pecan halves as a guide, cut the candy evenly into 1-inch squares.

Between layers of waxed paper, in a tightly covered container wrapped in several layers of aluminum foil, the squares will keep for 2 weeks in the refrigerator. They are best eaten at room temperature.

Fresh Fruit Jellies

Yield: 32 1-inch squares

Sparkling and clear, these fruit jellies are fun to make.

Ingredients

2 cups fresh raspberries

4 tablespoons (5 envelopes) unflavored powdered gelatin

1/4 cup cold water

1 cup sugar, divided

4 tablespoons light corn syrup

Line a baking sheet with aluminum foil, then place an 8-inch by 4 1/2-inch flan ring in the center of the foil. In a 2-quart heavy-bottomed saucepan over medium heat, heat the raspberries until they begin to release their juice (about 5 minutes), stirring constantly. Remove the pan from the heat and pour the raspberries into a strainer set over a bowl. With a wooden spoon, press through as much of the raspberry juice as possible. This should yield 2/3 cup raspberry juice.

In a small mixing bowl, dissolve the gelatin in the cold water. In a 2-quart heavy-bottomed saucepan over medium heat, combine the raspberry juice, 1/2 cup of the sugar, and corn syrup, and stir the mixture with a wooden spoon to dissolve the sugar. Add the softened gelatin and stir constantly until it dissolves completely (about 5 minutes). Remove the pan from the heat, and immediately turn the mixture onto the prepared flan ring. Let the candy set completely at room temperature (2 to 3 hours).

With the blade of a large chef's knife, loosen and remove the flan ring. Cut the candy across the width into 8 1-inch strips, then cut each strip into 4 pieces, forming 1-inch squares. Place the remaining 1/2 cup sugar in a round cake pan, roll each square in the sugar to coat it completely, then place each square in a paper candy cup. Between layers of waxed paper in a tightly covered container, the jellies will keep for 1 week at room temperature or 2 weeks in the refrigerator.

Substitute blackberries, strawberries, or blueberries for the raspberries. Substitute 2/3 cup freshly squeezed lemon or orange juice for the raspberries.

Glazed Fruit

Yield: 50 pieces

A sparkling coating of clear glaze enhances the beauty of fresh fruit. Because this glaze is fragile, the fruit must be eaten the same day it is prepared. Use only fruit that is perfectly ripe and unblemished, and make sure that the fruit is very dry before glazing, since humidity breaks down the glaze. A display of glazed fruit makes a stunning centerpiece for a buffet table or dinner party.

Ingredients

50 small pieces ripe fruit, such as strawberries, grapes, or cherries

1 large grapefruit

1 1/2 cups sugar

1/2 cup water

1/8 teaspoon cream of tartar

10 drops freshly squeezed lemon juice

Insert a toothpick or wooden skewer into the base of each small fruit. Cut off one end of the grapefruit to make a flat base, then pierce 50 small holes in the grapefruit, to hold the toothpicks for display. Line a baking sheet with a piece of waxed paper.

In a 2-quart heavy-bottomed saucepan over medium-high heat, bring the sugar, the water, and cream of tartar to a boil. Brush down the sides of the pan with a pastry brush dipped in warm water 2 times, to prevent the sugar from crystallizing. Cook the mixture until it registers 240°F on a sugar thermometer, then add the lemon juice. Brush down the sides of the pan 2 more times, and continue cooking the mixture until it registers 310°F on the thermometer.

Remove the pan from the heat. Holding a small fruit by the toothpick, dip the fruit into the sugar syrup, coating it completely. Lift the fruit from the syrup, gently shake off the excess syrup, and place the fruit onto the waxed paper. Repeat with the remaining small fruit. If the sugar syrup begins to firm up while you are working, warm it over medium heat until it is liquid again. Let the glaze set up at room temperature (about 10 minutes).

Place the toothpicks into the holes in the grapefruit, or place each piece of glazed fruit into a paper candy cup, and remove the toothpick.

Keep the fruit at room temperature until serving time. Serve the fruit within 12 hours of preparation.

Appendices

Table of Sugar Stages and Temperatures

A reliable candy/sugar thermometer is the best way to tell when sugar has cooked to the correct temperature. The following table indicates the stages that correspond to the temperature ranges of cooked sugar, the characteristics of each stage, and the uses for each stage. To test for these stages without a sugar thermometer, drop a teaspoonful of the sugar syrup into a glass of cold water then retrieve the syrup by pressing it between your thumb and forefinger.

Temperature Range	Stage	Characteristics and Uses
223-234°F	Thread	Forms a loose, thin thread. Used for sugar syrups.
234-240°F	Soft ball	Forms a soft, sticky ball that flattens when removed from the water. Used for fudge, caramels, and jam squares.
244-248°F	Firm ball	Forms a firm but pliable, sticky ball that holds its shape briefly, but deflates when left at room temperature for a few minutes. Used for caramels, Florentines, and nougat.
250-266°F	Hard ball	Forms a rigid, sticky ball that holds its shape against pressure. Used for caramels, nougat, divinity, and marmalade squares.
270-290°F	Soft crack	Separates into strands that are firm but pliable. Bite into a piece of the cooled syrup and it will stick to your teeth. Used for krokant, nougat, and torrone.
300-310°F	Hard crack	Separates into brittle threads that shatter easily. The sugar is no longer sticky. Used for brittles, toffee, and glazed fruit.
320-360°F	Caramel	Becomes transparent and undergoes color changes ranging from light golden to dark amber. Used for praline, brittles, nougatine, and buttercrunch.

Table of Weight & Measurement Equivalents

Chocolate

Ounces	Grams
1 ounce	15 grams
4 ounces (1/4 pound)	110 grams
8 ounces (1/2 pound)	230 grams
16 ounces (1 pound)	454 grams

Granulated Sugar

Measurement	Ounces	Grams
1 teaspoon	1/6 ounce	5 grams
1 tablespoon	1/2 ounce	15 grams
1/4 cup	1 3/4 ounces	50 grams
1/3 cup	2 1/4 ounces	65 grams
1/2 cup	3 1/2 ounces	100 grams
2/3 cup	4 1/2 ounces	130 grams
3/4 cup	5 ounces	150 grams
1 cup	7 ounces	200 grams

Brown Sugar

Measurement	Ounces	Grams
1 tablespoon	1/4 ounce	5 grams
1/4 cup	1 1/4 ounces	25 grams
1/3 cup	1 3/4 ounces	40 grams
1/2 cup	2 3/4 ounces	70 grams
2/3 cup	3 ounces	80 grams
3/4 cup	3 1/2 ounces	100 grams
1 cup	5 ounces	145 grams

Corn Syrup, Honey, Molasses, Maple Syrup

Measurement	Fluid Ounces	Ounces by Weight	Grams
2 tablespoons	1 fluid ounce	1 1/4 ounces	25 grams
1/4 cup	2 fluid ounces	3 1/2 ounces	100 grams
1/3 cup	3 fluid ounces	4 1/2 ounces	130 grams
1/2 cup	4 fluid ounces	6 1/2 ounces	170 grams
2/3 cup	5 fluid ounces	8 ounces	225 grams
3/4 cup	6 fluid ounces	9 1/2 ounces	250 grams
1 cup	8 fluid ounces	12 ounces	340 grams

Nuts

Weight of 1 cup, shelled	Ounces	Grams
Almonds, sliced	3 ounces	85 grams
Cashews	4 1/2 ounces	130 grams
Hazelnuts	4 1/2 ounces	130 grams
Macadamia nuts	4 ounces	110 grams
Peanuts	4 ounces	110 grams
Pecans	4 ounces	110 grams
Pistachio nuts	5 ounces	150 grams
Walnuts	3 1/2 ounces	100 grams

Butter

Measurement	Ounces	Grams
1 tablespoon	1/2 ounce	15 grams
2 tablespoons	1 ounce	30 grams
4 tablespoons (1/2 stick, 1/4 cup)	2 ounces	60 grams
8 tablespoons (1 stick, 1/2 cup)	4 ounces (1/4 pound)	115 grams
2 sticks	8 ounces (1/2 pound)	230 grams
4 sticks	1 pound	454 grams

Liquid Measurements

Measurement	Equivalent
1/4 cup (2 fluid ounces)	4 tablespoons
1/3 cup (3 fluid ounces)	5 tablespoons
1/2 cup (4 fluid ounces)	8 tablespoons
2/3 cup (5 fluid ounces)	10 tablespoons
3/4 cup (6 fluid ounces)	12 tablespoons
1 cup (8 fluid ounces)	16 tablespoons

Dry Measurements

Measurement	Equivalent
3 teaspoons	1 tablespoon
2 tablespoons	1/8 cup
4 tablespoons	1/4 cup
5 tablespoons	1/3 cup
8 tablespoons	1/2 cup
16 tablespoons	1 cup

Weight Equivalents

1/2 pound = 230 grams   1 pound = 454 grams   1 kilo = 2.2 pounds

INDEX